GAME ON! ENDORSEMENTS

"Everyone who influences another person is a coach. Coaches are disciples and coaches disciple others. In *Game On*, Jay presents a biblically based game plan to help all coaches elevate their game. It's a message that is delivered in a practical, entertaining, and memorable way. Whether you enjoy athletics or not, you and those you lead will benefit if you transfer these lessons to your life."
—Dabo Swinney, Head Football Coach, Clemson University

"Jay displays a grace in his writing that is consistent with his personality. It conveys the distinct clarity of his commitment to Christ, while still being inviting to those who may not have yet received Christ as their Savior. I found it interesting how he was able to biblically leverage stories so as to make them strategic in advancing kingdom purposes. *Game On* is about maximizing our talents through obedience and the opportunities we are presented in this lifetime. Jay recognizes that this cannot occur apart from Jesus. I believe this book can help coaches reevaluate their goals, motivation, strategy for culture, and definition of success. It can help them cast a biblical worldview in their coaching, as well as their personal lives. In my opinion, any book considered great in this world written by man, woman, or child—is a book that will invite and drive the reader to God's Word—the Bible. I'm trusting and believing that *Game On* will do that for you. I wholeheartedly endorse Jay's efforts to present Jesus to all coaches—both those within and outside of the realm of sports—so they might know Jesus and make him known to others."
—Ron Brown, Co-Founder, Kingdom Sports Ministry

i

"All Christ followers benefit from proven coaching principles. And that's exactly what you'll get from Jay Mills in *Game On!* This relatable and entertaining book is a novel approach, sure to boost your spiritual momentum. Everyone who is serious about their faith will find practical help in this playbook. Don't miss out on Jay's game plan and incredible wisdom."

—Dr. Les Parrott, #1 *New York Times* bestselling author

"In *Game On! A Coach's Game Plan for Discipleship*, Pastor/Coach Jay Mills provides timely insight and a resource for every "coach"— whether in athletics, ministry, or business—who wants to provide transformational leadership in their sphere of influence. Jay's words and guidance come from his real life experience as a head football coach who lived the instruction he writes of. The practical biblical truths of Pastor Mills' book offer any size study group of Christ-followers an essential tool for spiritual growth and formation."

—Dr. Rick Brewer, President, Louisiana College

"One of the most comprehensive biblically based books that integrates scripture with practical applications of coaching that I have ever read. The biblical game plan presented transcends sports and provides a great resource for today's Christian journey."

—Jim Caldwell, Former Head Coach, Indianapolis Colts & Detroit Lions

"Game On!" is a well-organized game plan that will help transform Christ followers into "coaching Christians." This book not only assists athletic coaches who are Christians, it encourages all disciples to apply coaching principles in their lives. I recommend it to everyone who desires to compete and win the game of life!"

—Dal Shealy, Past President of the Fellowship of Christian Athletes

"You don't have to be a coach, or even a sports enthusiast, to benefit from Jay's insights. If you're a follower of Jesus Christ, and want to help expand the kingdom, this book is a must-read. It not only provides the coaching you need to benefit you but it helps you live a victorious Christian life as well."
—Albert Long-motivational speaker-author, FCA Hall of Fame Inductee

"Jay Mills' *Game On! A Coach's Game Plan For Discipleship* is a great balance of a systematic approach, filled with great real-life examples, illustrations, stories, and motivation; inspiring us all to take the Christian life beyond ourselves. He has carefully and thoughtfully outlined and backed-up the true recipe for being a Christ follower who intends on living the Christian life as a giver, not a taker; written for the coach by the coach. The stories, followed by lessons just flow and it's obvious in just the first few paragraphs that you'll be both encouraged and challenged as a believer and leader/coach. As a Christian you'll also be guided through the steps of giving yourself away. Jay provides compelling evidence for the art and system of coaching. Any Christian can benefit from this thoughtful, funny, and challenging book. Be prepared however, he does not pull any punches, he doesn't shy away from the hard challenges; this is the real deal."
—Brent Ives, Principal, BHI Management Consulting

"One of the unique things about athletes is they want to be coached – even *coached hard* as elite athletes often say. They want someone as a guide and mentor, as well as someone who will confront them and demand excellence. Disciples should be like that – eagerly accepting the challenge to continual spiritual growth and personal development. This book combines the best principles of coaching and life-changing discipleship. If you are an athlete – or not – this book will inspire and motivate you to pursue excellence in your relationships with God and others."
—Jeff Iorg, President, Gateway Seminary

"*Game On!* is an excellent, succinct tool for guiding us on our discipleship path. Jay's smooth writing style combines the perfect balance of wit and wisdom as he presents a clear path by which we can each fulfill our destiny of becoming a Christian coach. While we may not coach a sports team, Jay shows us not only our responsibility to coach those God has placed in our care, but the means by which we can do so effectively. Jay uses strong biblical teaching, combined with engaging and entertaining stories, to motivate us to action and to illustrate techniques for sharing the message of Christ that invoke personal growth both for us and those we coach."
—Julie Bennett, VP Bristol Motor Speedway

"In *Game On!*, Jay Mills distills decades of hard won wisdom from both coaching and church ministry experience into a fresh perspective on life transformation for Christian coaches. Asserting that "every Christ follower is a coach," Jay unpacks a vision and a plan to utilize coaching insights in developing disciples, both in personal and church ministry settings. Read *Game On!* to learn how you can pass on both a message and a skill set to those God gives you the privilege of coaching."
—Dr. Mike Nolen, Lead Pastor at Southwinds Church, Past President of the California Southern Baptist Convention, and former Chairman of the Board of Trustees for California Baptist University

"When you combine a deep-rooted faith in Jesus Christ with the heart for leadership and loving people – you get Jay Mills. Jay weaves the foundational pieces of Christ centered leadership with a coaching expertise that gives a road map to bringing others into that space. His desire to see hearts led and aligned with Jesus Christ shines through and provides wonderful examples of "Coaching the Game of Life!"
—Mitch Barnhart, Director of Athletics, University of Kentucky, and past national advisory board member of K-Love Radio

GAME ON!

A Coach's Game Plan For Discipleship

JAY MILLS

To my beautiful wife, Kim – – I am blessed to be your husband.

CONTENTS

FOREWORD

Coaching is not just a vocation, and it's not just a hobby; it's a way of life and a calling. I coached college football for forty-five years, but my coaching career did not come to a close when the clock struck zero in that final game; I've continued to coach off the field. This is the point Jay Mills makes in *Game On! A Coach's Game Plan For Discipleship*. You, too, are a coach. In your family, community, workplace and at your church, in whatever role you have, wherever you reside and wherever your journey takes you, you can make a positive contribution in the lives of others. As Jay says: "Coaches transform and coaches transport."

In a society that constantly focuses on rights and privileges, we must remember that leadership is about responsibilities and obligations—and that begins with our faith. Our transformation as disciples of Jesus Christ should be our ultimate objective. This book helps you concentrate on that transformational goal.

I don't believe you can accomplish an awful lot in life, anything worthwhile, without a faith in God and I can't believe that God put us on this earth to be ordinary. Jay believes that as well. Jay was a member of my first coaching staff at the University of Notre Dame in 1986. Since then, I've followed his career as both a college football coach and as a pastor. One thing I know is that whatever he's done, he has done it for the right reasons.

In *Game On*, Jay combines experiences from thirty years of coaching with many hours of biblical study to present practical ways to apply faith for your personal growth and those you mentor—and he has done it in an enlightening, unique and entertaining way. I'm confident that you will benefit from the wisdom he shares.

God has given us a lot of power—power to love, think, create, imagine, plan—but the greatest power we have is the power to choose. I think life is a matter of choices and that wherever we are, good or bad, it's because of choices we make. The world is in need of coaches in every facet of life to help people choose well.

Coaches transport. So true. I believe you can have anything you want in life if you help enough people get what they want. I want my time on this earth to count, and that is not calculated by the number of wins on my coaching record. For victory in life, we've got to keep focused on the goal, and the goal is Heaven. And it's not just for our sake.

On the field and off, coaches influence those around them. On the sideline, the players usually are going to reflect the atmosphere that is generated by their coach. If the coach doesn't have much faith, your players usually will reflect that. This is indicative in the game of life as well. Coaches must have faith. I believe the impact you have as a coaching leader runs deeper and wider into how people live their lives and in turn impact others. Jay shares that you are a branch on a coaching tree and from your shoot you grow your own coaching tree. We are all disciples who make disciples, so we must not take our role lightly.

Coaching gives one a chance to be successful as well as significant. We can all be successful and make money, but when we die, that ends. But when you are significant is when you help other people be successful. That lasts many a lifetime—and when you concentrate on matters of faith, it will last many an eternity!

Jay contends that this requires a game plan and I wholeheartedly agree. Sacrifice, discipline and prayer are essential. We gain strength through God's word. And when we fumble due to sin—and it's gonna happen—confession puts us back on the field. These are just a few of the components this book conveys in this game plan for life. In the pages which follow, there are also coaching points on delayed gratification, teamwork, communication, lessons on overcoming adversity, and many other important topics.

I believe that having a spiritual life is so important in everybody's life and that we all benefit from coaching. I know that others influenced my life tremendously by encouraging me to always make sure that God was the focus of my life. Jay not only echoes this sentiment, but he also lays out a pathway for how we can pay it forward.

In our life's journey, when we do the right thing, do the best we can, and show others that we care, we become the coach we were meant to be, and we help others do the same. As Jay points out, we have opportunities all around us—sometimes we just don't recognize them.

We all have twenty-four hours a day, sixty minutes to an hour and sixty seconds to a minute; it's how we spend them that is really important. Don't be a spectator, don't let life pass you by. The key to winning is choosing to do God's will and loving others with all you've got. Read *Game On!* and learn the pathway to victory in coaching the game of life.

Lou Holtz

Hall of Fame Coach and recipient of the
Presidential Medal of Freedom

ACKNOWLEDGMENTS

Thirty years ago, while I was driving on I-5 between Tacoma and Seattle, I heard the Lord tell me I needed to write a book. It wasn't an audible voice, but it provided a sense of unmistakable direction, nonetheless. Oswald Chambers once said that a person realizes their calling from God with "a sudden thunderclap or with a gradual dawning, but in whatever way it comes it comes with the undercurrent of the supernatural, something that cannot be put into words." This is that book. Please do not follow my example and wait three decades before you obediently answer what you have been called to do!

To paraphrase a friend of mine, "there are a lot of reasons, not one valid excuse for not doing what we've been called to do." So, after much delay, I set out on this journey. I spent six months compiling information, sorted it topically, and then prayerfully organized the material in preparation for writing. I think I could have continued this leg of the journey indefinitely. However, I heard that voice once again, and it told me it was time to put pen to the paper. I'll never forget sitting in front of my laptop staring at a blank Word document, which appeared to be staring back at me, and wondering: "Am I even going to be able to write one sentence?"

By the grace of God, not only have I completed my assignment, I have a second book nearly ready for release. In addition, each month I distribute a newsletter, *Coaching Points*. Stay tuned for more! I did not set out to become an author and writer, but on my life journey, I've found God to be the Lord of redirection. For me, Solomon's words ring loud and true: "In their hearts humans plan their course, but the Lord establishes their steps" (Proverbs 16:9).

At every fork in the road, the Lord has reassured me: "Whether you turn to the right or to the left, your ears will hear a voice behind you, saying, 'This is the way; walk in it" (Isaiah 30:21). Just make sure that His voice is heard. The Lord has placed a number of individuals in my life to amplify His message and ensure I stay on the right path. The voices that have guided me belong to family members, friends, student-athletes, coaches, pastors, and others. The length of our association has varied, but all have been seasons I have treasured and each word exchanged has been crucial in bringing me to this day. There is a Turkish proverb that states: "No road is long with good company." I've been so honored to have great traveling companions from the outset—beginning with my parents.

Charles Swindoll said that parents should provide their children with "roots and wings." They must train them so that they will possess a root system that will enable them to be strong when they are exposed to the inclement atmospheric conditions of life. Parents should also allow their children to sprout their wings and go where the Lord leads. My parents, Jay and Jan Mills, gave each of their four sons roots and wings. My mom made sure that our home was rooted in Jesus Christ, God centered and Spirit led. Although she has gone through some very challenging times, I've never seen her faith waiver. To this day, she continues to provide a consistent Christlike example. My dad was the greatest coach I've ever known. Someone once said, "the speed of the leaders determines the rate of the pack." When it comes to work ethic, perseverance, toughness and discipline, my dad set a world-record pace. My brothers and I are still trying to catch up.

My brothers, Jeff, Jerry, and Joby are good men, husbands and fathers. What a testament they are to the important role of parents and how love, support, and respect can be transferred from one generation to the next. Each of these men are devoted to their church and successful professionally. Not only have they inspired me, but they have also provided me with some pretty humorous stories to share with others! #keepreading!

Kim and I have a total of six children and five grandchildren (let me assure you, the headcount for the children won't change, but I'm confident more grandchildren will be on the way). This book is dedicated to one person, but it was motivated by our children, their spouses, and the grandkids. If this book can bring them a small fraction of the joy they bring me, I will consider this book a great success.

I'm grateful for the extended family I have in Arkansas, Texas, and Iowa. There are lessons conveyed in these pages that originate with the influence of my grandparents, aunts, uncles and cousins. Some of them have passed, but cherished memories will always remain. There are way too many of them to mention by name—and the list continues to grow. In fact, day by day, I'm becoming more convinced that I'm somehow related to just about everyone in Northwest Arkansas! Warren Weirsbe says, "The only way to end up with the right destination is to choose the right road." My family put me on the right road, but there are a number of others who have kept me on the correct track.

I want to thank all the student athletes, coaching colleagues, and assistant coaches who served on my staff over the years. I was so blessed to work with so many fine individuals at Central Catholic High School (Bloomington, IL), Western Washington University, the University of Notre Dame, Boise State University, University of Minnesota (Morris, MN), Harvard University and Charleston Southern University. A number of stories that I share come from these experiences and relationships.

I could not have transferred these valuable lessons to others had I not been able to serve under some tremendous head coaches. John McIntyre gave me my start in this wonderful profession. Gerry Faust hired me at Notre Dame and gave me the opportunity to get my master's degree from this excellent institution, while demonstrating true humility from a very visible position. Skip Hall not only added me to his staff at Boise State, I got to watch him integrate his Christian faith into his role. Tim Murphy afforded me the opportunity to serve at the most prestigious university in the world (Harvard), while providing me with an organizational template I would apply as well as a head coach and in vocational ministry.

There are two additional head coaches and one athletic director I want to specifically thank: Lou Holtz, Paul Hansen, and Hank Small. When there was a transition in the coaching staff at Notre Dame, Coach Holtz gave me the opportunity to remain at the university and serve on his staff. That was December 2, 1985. There is not a day that has gone by since, that his influence has not been incorporated in what I do. His name occurs more than once in the pages that follow, but his presence permeates throughout this book.

I met Paul Hansen when he served briefly as my quarterback coach at Illinois State University. Although we only spent a couple of months together, I was so impressed with this Christian man that, when he offered me an opportunity to join his staff at Western Washington, I moved sight unseen to the great Northwest for a grand total of $2300/year! In addition to being my mentor and chief encourager, Paul has been my closest friend since 1983. Through every up and down, Paul has been by my side. I owe Paul a debt of gratitude that I truly can never repay.

For a decade, Hank Small served as my Athletic Director at Charleston Southern, but our relationship began years earlier. As they say, there's only two types of coaches: those who have been fired and those who will be fired! When I was unemployed, Hank called me every week for months to see how I was doing. Here's what was incredible: Until then, we only saw each other once a year at a coach's convention. I will never forgot the grace he displayed to me and my family. Years later, when he offered me the head coaching job at Charleston Southern, I jumped at the chance to be with Hank. Not only did we work well together, but I also benefited from the wise Christian leadership of this man.

I wish to thank the pastors that have poured into me as well: Bob Hines, Mike Sager, David Platt (no, not that one), Stan Cruse, Eric Lethco, Keith Sharp and Jon Davis. These men coached me while I was a lay member of their church; their influence continues to guide me as a pastor and writer. Now, in vocational ministry, I've also been privileged to serve under three excellent lead pastors: Mickey Rainwater, Mike Nolen, and Jamus Edwards. Each has helped shape my theology, which is apparent in my ordained role and in the books and articles I author.

My wife says it takes at least two women to run my life. Later, she said, "I stand corrected; it takes at least three!" I'm so appreciative the ladies that have, figuratively, carried me over the years: Beth Myers, Paula Callahan, Sue Ann Greene, Becci Ciraulo, Debbie Knapp, Rene Snyder, and Debbie Molloy. In addition, there are two women who were vital in launching the CJM (Coach Jay Mills) ministry: Madeline Zelmer and Adrienne Doppee. These fine women love the Lord and they serve Him wholeheartedly. You'll never know what a blessing you've been to me.

There is one assistant I would like to single out: Jennifer Dabalos. From the outset, this sister in Christ has encouraged and supported me in this endeavor. I would do her a disservice to attempt to name everything she has done on my behalf and for our ministry—the list is just too extensive. Let me just simply and sincerely say: "Thank you Jennifer."

There are so many others, dear friends, such as Dr. Rick Brewer, Dr. Mary Papke, Neil Rose, Emmett Morgan, Dal Shealy, Mark Warren, Fred Raines, Ron Brown, Wally Sparks, Brent and Lynda Ives, Tim and Pam Steger, Dick and Sherry Arbuckle, and Laura Spoon. This book simply could not have been written without the friendship and the mentoring they have given me. Your influence impacted me directly and indirectly helped me write this book.

I'm truly grateful for those who helped me illustrate, edit and promote this book. I appreciate the artistic abilities Hannah Linder displayed in creating the cover of the book, and Rene Snyder's meaningful illustrations within the book's cover. Meredith Brown has faithfully walked with me on this journey for over four years by serving as the primary editor. Jim Watkins led me through three rewrites, while serving as the content editor. I learned so much from this veteran. Finally, line editor, Linda Au, put the finishing touches on this piece. Lastly, I am grateful for Mike Carleton and the staff at 42nd St., which created and hosts my website: coachjaymills.com. Their creativeness and professionalism is truly top-notch.

If you've ever attempted to write a book, then you know the value of obtaining agent representation. Like most first-time authors, my query letters received one reject letter after another. However, there was one person who believed in me: Jim Hart. I signed a contract with the prestigious Hartline Literary Agency in the spring of 2020. Since then, Jim has become more than my agent; he is my friend.

Last but not least, the love of my life: Kim Mills. I regularly tell "K," that the Lord has blessed her with "beauty and brains," but I am the benefactor of this blessing. I have never met such a caring individual, who also possesses such spiritual wisdom. Her demeanor is quiet and subtle, but her influence is larger-than-life. She is a prayer warrior, who possesses a servant's heart. Everyone she meets draws close to her, because she selflessly focuses on the needs of others rather than herself. In turbulent times, her steady presence brings tranquility.

During one the most difficult stretches in this process, my wife artistically created a small sign that she set on the edge of our desk: "Never be lacking in zeal, but keep your spiritual fervor, serving the Lord. Be joyful in hope, patient in affliction, faithful in prayer" (Romans 12:11 – 12).

Her walk matches her talk; what you see is what you get. As Peter said, husbands "may be won without a word by the conduct of their wives, when they see your respectful and pure conduct" (1 Peter 3:1 – 2). She won me over early on and she continues to do so on a daily basis. Even when we're apart, I carry a reminder of her devotion. On the inside of my wedding band, Kim transcribed the following: "Our journey; our testimony." From beginning until the end, we are in this together. I am truly privileged to walk alongside this special woman on life's journey.

There is simply no way for me to thank everyone who has impacted me over this span of time. To paraphrase the apostle John, if every name were written down, I suppose that the list would become a book in itself. However, please know that I am truly grateful and so humbled by the investment you have made. Without your contributions, that Word document would still be blank.

1

COACHING THE GAME OF LIFE

"The words I speak are not my own, but my Father who lives in me does His work through me."

John 14:10

Whether it was in our childhood, adolescence, or adulthood, we all learned valuable life lessons from the world of sports.

Analogies between sports and life are frequently referenced in Scripture. When describing how a Christ follower could live a Spirit-filled life, Paul spoke of the runner, the wrestler, and the boxer. However, the stake in the game is greater for the Christ follower than those of the athlete. We are not competing for the laurel wreath that fades, it's a matter of life and death! There is an adversary who wants not only to defeat us but to eternally destroy us (1 Corinthians 9:25). And so, Christian coaching is critical to helping Christ followers win the game of life.

Like Jesus' words above, the goal of this book is "not my words," but only my story. My prayer and quest have been to be a faithful messenger; to testify of lessons learned from thirty years of coaching and apply it to coaching believers to succeed in their personal and professional lives. Coaching is a metaphor for discipleship, a leadership model, and a transferable skill set. It provides a non-cookie-cutter approach to ministry and mission that is applicable in all your endeavors.

Christian Coaching is the method in which we fulfill our purpose and answer our calling. We may wear many hats and be located on a variety of job sites, but our work gloves look the same. To be a "Christian" coach means that we are to implement biblical principles for our eternal benefit and the everlasting benefit of others. We are being changed, and we are to lead others along a similar path of spiritual improvement. It is an indisputable charge for those who profess Jesus Christ to be their Lord and Savior. You were created to coach.

We Transform and Transport

From theory to application, Christian coaches accomplish two primary objectives: we transform and transport. We assist in life transformation and we help our followers in their journey until one day we both kneel before the heavenly throne.

One of the first lessons the Lord taught me was this: my job is to prepare; the Lord's job is to promote—and always in His timing. To assist others on this spiritual journey, the Lord provided a number of unique experiences throughout my coaching tenure to equip me to share what He wants promoted.

I served at a high school and in every level in the strata of college football. I served Protestant, Catholic, public and private schools and was associated with the two major organizations that govern intercollegiate sports: the NCAA and the NAIA.

Now, I believe God provided circumstances for a greater purpose: to help believers achieve victory in the game of life.

Maybe you took the field years ago but have become disappointed as the game of life progressed. Or maybe you are just setting out training for the race. You are looking for a life coach to help guide you—especially on the unknown course ahead. To you, the path appears to be unmarked. You have good intentions, but what you need are clear markers.

If you can relate, then this book is written for you, so that you might be encouraged.

"Give strength to hands that are tired and to knees that tremble with weakness. Tell everyone who is discouraged, 'Be strong and don't be afraid! God is coming to your rescue'" (Isaiah 35:3-4 GNT).

This book is intended to present a fresh perspective to help you to, not just stay in the game, but to take the trophy Christ has promised.

We're on the Same Team

Regardless of the sport, in the coaching profession, colleagues are typically very guarded with their schemes. Because of their competitive nature, they do not divulge their professional secrets to just anyone; they believe it might just negate their advantage and compromise their ability to win.

As a Christian coach, we hold nothing back. We are all emissaries of one God and members of the same team. Together, we all win. I experienced many victories over my athletic coaching career—and many defeats as well—and I was blessed with treasured memories that I still reflect upon from time to time. I coached a Heisman Trophy winner, and I was even the head coach for a team that set a national record! Before you become impressed, I must confess that the record we set was that of the biggest underdog in the history of college football. And I witnessed the most unusual meeting in the history of the game.

Our Ultimate Objective

As I made my way from the press box to the sideline at Birmingham's Legion Field, just before halftime, the chant of the crowd became louder and more deafening with each step I took. "Roll Tide! Roll Tide!"

If it continued its crescendo, dogs would soon begin to howl and every glass in the vicinity would shatter! It was my third season at the University of Notre Dame and my first under new head football coach, Lou Holtz. Although I was still a novice in the coaching profession, that day would leave an indelible mark in my tutelage under this future Hall of Fame coach.

As a defensive assistant, my role was to proceed to the locker room just prior to halftime in order to prepare analysis on Alabama's offensive tendencies. This would allow our defensive staff to make the necessary alterations to put us in the best position for success in the second half. I decided to make my way to our sideline to watch our offense attempt a "two-minute" drive before halftime. The passion from the fans in the stands was met with an equally impressive intensity from the Alabama defense. When I got to our team's bench, my front-row vantage gave me access to a perspective that the audience at home just did not have. And what I saw startled me.

The speed and tenacity at which the Crimson Tide's defensive front pressured our quarterback was a sight to behold. I have always believed that it is important to be grateful in life and, at that moment, I was grateful that I was not our quarterback! Legendary football coach Tommy Prothro once said, "Quarterbacks and receivers are the toughest individuals in the game, because they never know where the hit is coming from," but I knew—it was coming from two individuals on the Crimson Tide defensive line. What I did not know, however, was that Alabama's edge rushers would later become NFL Hall of Fame inductees. Cornelius Bennett and Derrick Thomas. They pursued our quarterback with speed, strength, and agility and wanted one thing and our quarterback was in possession of it.

As the clock wound down, our offense came up short, but at least our quarterback maintained possession of the ball—as well as all of his body parts—until both squads exited the field for the traditional twenty-minute recess.

As amazed as I was at the Alabama team's athletic prowess, still it was nothing compared to what I witnessed in the Notre Dame locker room that afternoon. Coach Holtz's halftime response was unconventional and truly enlightening, especially to this twenty-four-year-old aspiring coach.

Typically, the offensive staff and defensive coaching staff would conduct their first-half review, and second-half preparations independently from one another. But on this day, Coach Holtz convened a full staff meeting in private quarters. "Men, we're not going to fix this in one half." The elephant in the room had been addressed and the reality of our situation was succinctly summarized.

With that comment still echoing in the room, he told the staff to "make sure your players play hard in the second half." He then devoted the rest of the time exclusively to how we would recruit for the future of the program. No other mention was made to our opponent. No schematic adjustments; no personnel changes. Nothing.

I had never heard before or since, a halftime discussion like this one. As you might have guessed, we didn't fare much better in the second half, losing to the second-ranked Crimson Tide, 28-0, but the effort level of the squad never subsided.

Coach Holtz wanted to win that game as much as anyone, but defeating Alabama that day was not the overarching theme on his agenda. His ultimate objective was to win the national championship. Brilliantly, he knew what needed

> *Great coaches foresee what is required and don't hesitate to move those they lead in a new direction.*

to be done and when it needed to occur. Great coaches foresee what is required and don't hesitate to move those they lead in a new direction. They're not afraid to try a new track—even if the new rails have never been ridden before. In this instance, we needed to get off that track and on another ASAP! Are you tracking with me? Every moment counts and Coach Holtz was determined not to waste a minute; it did not take long before his gamble paid off. Two years later, Notre Dame would conclude a perfect 12-0 season and be crowned national champions. To this day, I am still convinced that championship was birthed in the locker room on that unique Saturday afternoon.

The prophet Isaiah writes about new tracks. "And a highway shall be there, and it shall be called the Way of Holiness; the unclean shall not pass over it. It shall belong to those who walk on the way" (Isaiah 35:8 ESV).

Coaches don't keep running the same play if it is ineffective; they try a new approach! To paraphrase the well-known words from *Star Trek,* the Christ follower needs five essentials to boldly go where he or she has never gone before: A new message, a new route, a new light, a new guide, and a new role.

If we are to set out on a new route, we must be willing to move in a new direction, dismiss what we previously relied upon, and look to someone who can safely lead us there. In short, we need a coach, and we must be willing to be coached. Furthermore, as we begin our journey, we need a well-lit path to enhance our vision and illuminate our course. For the Christian coach, "the old is gone, the new has come" (2 Corinthians 5:17 GNT), and new details are always forthcoming.

A New Message

One of the ways we know that it's God who is speaking to us is that the message is counterintuitive; it's unlike anything else we hear. Our Master Coach's game plan and instructions can occasionally seem peculiar and opposite of our natural inclination, but we should listen and comply.

For instance: "But to you who are listening I say: Love your enemies, do good to those who hate you, bless those who curse you, pray for those who mistreat you. If someone slaps you on the cheek, turn to them the other also. If someone takes your coat, do not withhold your shirt from them" (Luke 6:27-29).

Who does this? If we are obedient, then the answer is you and me. Only by the grace of God, can we possibly aspire to live in such a lofty manner.

These principles contrast with the message dispatched by the world and easily distinguish a mindset not originated by man. Embracing such a philosophy is sure to put us, as well as those with whom we are called to share this ideology, in the minority. To paraphrase Robert Frost's famous poem, *The Road Not Taken,* two roads diverged in the wood; the Christian coach takes the one less traveled--and that makes all the difference.

A New Route

Since the time of Adam and Eve, humankind's existence has begun with an inward focus, which produces outward actions based on instincts, trial and error, and self-sufficiency. The Book of Judges states it in this way: "In those days there was no king in Israel; every man did what was right in his own eyes" (Judges 17:6 NASB).

Today, that pattern of behavior is still the norm. Overwhelmingly, men and women turn to themselves and their own intellect and judgment but, as Solomon warns, their interpretation can bring about devastating consequences: "There is a way that appears to be right, but in the end it leads to death" (Proverbs 14:12).

For some, it might take a near-death experience to seek a new way, but it need not. Thankfully, God's grace provides ample opportunities for us to divert our course, but one key question still remains: Will we heed the warnings?

My dad was always looking for new paths. Whenever my brothers and I get together, we laugh as we respectfully recall one of our father's patented phrases, "I found a new blacktop; a diagonal that provides a better way." Isn't that what we are all looking for? A better way?

We should never criticize one who carves out a new pathway that eases our travels. Like my earthly father, our Heavenly Father will occasionally take us somewhere we have never gone and to get there He will lead us on a path we have never traveled. When God called Abraham to "Go," he set out on a road for a land that was foreign to him. The Lord would shine His light on Abraham and illuminate a pathway for him to follow, and He extends an offer for similar passage to each of us today.

Is there something that you have sensed that you should do, but the thought of it was so outlandish that you denied yourself even imagining the possibility? Go! If we think we are too far-gone and that the Lord could not possibly use us, we need only remember Abraham. Like him, the Lord can construct a new route to take us from our humble beginnings and put us on the road to prosperity. We need only follow a new path and look to the light.

A New Light

When we travel in darkness, we are only able to see a portion of the road ahead. As we successfully navigate that part of our passage, more of the route becomes exposed. Eventually, we will see all we need to see as we incrementally move forward.

Sometimes, the Lord will shine His light to announce His presence and invite us to join Him. Other times, He will bring the darkness to stir a desire within us to seek His guiding light. The burning bush helped Moses to "see the light" (Exodus 3). Conversely, it was through this enlightened servant that the Lord brought a plague that centered on the absence of light. Moses had tried to reason with the Pharaoh, but as Angela Duckworth writes, "Lectures don't have half the effect of consequences." If you are in the dark today, choose not to remain there; look to Jesus Christ, the Light that "shines on in the darkness, and the darkness has never put it out" (John 1:5 ISV).

Following the Light means that we not only seek divine guidance for direction, but we desire to move forward mirroring the same moral purity and ethical example that Christ displayed. Although we will come up short time and time again, nevertheless, we strive to travel the road to perfection by abiding in our Savior and embracing God's Word. In doing so, His light shines through us onto others so that the lumens of God's grace and mercy in the world are magnified.

One day at a time, one step at a time, "I will lead the blind by ways they have not known, along unfamiliar paths I will guide them; I will turn the darkness into light before them and make the rough places smooth. These are the things I will do; I will not forsake them" (Isaiah 42:16).

When given the chance to enlighten us, those around us may opt in or opt out, but not the Lord. The Lord promises to always be there to shed some light, not only on the subject matter but on each of us; we are His subjects and the focus of His projection. Psalm 27 first uses light as a metaphor for God. His illumination makes sure we are on the right road, prevents us from getting off course, and makes visible those on our path with whom He intends us to intersect. When we look to the Lord for guidance, He makes the correct path evident.

A New Guide

As absurd as some of the Lord's requests might seem at times, the results speak for themselves. Who would have ever thought that marching around a city and blowing a trumpet would be a successful strategy in breaking down the impenetrable walls of Jericho? Could you ever conceive that the youngest of Jesse's sons, still tending to his father's sheep, would be qualified to become king? Or could you believe that the Lord would reprove Balaam's path by enabling a donkey to speak? But, if that is what needs to happen so a Christ follower stays the course, the Lord will speak by whatever means necessary.

For the Christian coach, there is a new message, a new route, and a new light supported by a perfect and timeless warranty; His methods are often unconventional, but His results are guaranteed. Our Guide is the foremost authority on any subject, the expert in any field. If we are hungry for answers, David says there is no need to avert our eyes and suppress our appetite. "The eyes of all look to you, and you give them their food at the proper time" (Psalm 145:15).

> *For the Christian coach, there is a new message, a new route, and a new light supported by a perfect and timeless warranty; His methods are often unconventional, but His results are guaranteed.*

Rations for the Journey

For our sustenance, literally and figuratively, the Lord will sometimes assign unfamiliar tasks and lead us to the most unlikely of individuals and places.

As we see in the story of the prophet Elijah providing the widow of Zarephath an ever-full jar of flour and jug of oil (1 Kings 17:7-16), the Lord might take us to a place of scarcity so that we might learn a valuable life lesson. As Watchman Nee once said, "Because of our proneness to look at the bucket and forget the fountain, God has to frequently change His means of supply to keep our eyes fixed on the source." We are to look and lean upon Him each and every day.

But, the woman in Zarephath wasn't the only widow to learn what God can do with limited rations. A widow, who was faced with having her two sons taken as slaves to satisfy a debt, pleads to Elisha. The prophet instructed her to gather up all the empty jars she could find, and God filled each and every one with valuable olive oil from her one small jar— enough to pay the debt! (2 Kings 4:1-7)

The moral of both stories is to rely on the Lord for our daily provision. Regardless of whether there is a surplus or no extra rations, the Lord will always fill our empty vessels and make our little go a long way! If and when your back is against the wall, "It ain't over till it's over." God will keep the oil flowing and replenish our reserve. We can confidently go where He leads, because we will have what we need when we need it.

A New Role

While Lou Holtz needed a staff of assistant coaches to implement his plan, the Lord doesn't need an entourage to get the job done. Still, He invites us to partner with Him in His redemptive plan for a lost world. He has begun a process in us that promises to propel us on an adventure and a job description for us to implement as we travel.

"So now Israel, what do you think God expects from you? Just this: live in His presence in holy reverence, follow the road He sets out for you, love Him, serve God, your God, with everything you have in you" (Deuteronomy 10:12 MSG).

What a privilege and what a responsibility. From the starting line to the finish line, and as we progress on the line in between; it is an honor to move forward on His behalf.

Everyone has a purpose, and one of our purposes is to intervene on behalf of others. Annie Dupre, front person for the Annie Moses Band, describes it this way, "We are all on a road. We are either prodigals; running away from our Heavenly Father or children running into His open arms." To lead people in the right direction, we must first be willing to go there ourselves. Somebody has to point the way; someone must lead the procession. The world is in need of Christian coaches. The world needs you.

New and Improved

Everyone seeks out a better way and, whether they realize it or not, our subconscious is triggered by anything that promotes the possibility. Marketers know "new and improved" will appeal to our senses. If we trust the one who is making the claim, we willingly follow along—and we do not hesitate to get going.

As Jon Acuff says, "Initiation is more important than preparation." Abraham and the two widows were repeatedly told to "Go!" And God's Word tells us to be alert for new and improved pathways as well: "Forget about what happened; don't keep going over old history. Be alert, be present. I'm about to do something brand-new. It's bursting out! Don't you see it? There it is! I'm making a road through the desert, rivers in the badlands" (Isaiah 43:18-19 MSG).

There is no such thing as an easy way, and some training is harder than others, but we must trust our Master Coach. There is an undeniable parallel between this reality and the words Christ spoke to Peter that someone will "lead you where you do not want to go" (John 21:18). Like Peter, if we have our choice, we would have never chosen the same route. But also, like Peter, "Surely not, Lord" (Acts 10:14) is vernacular that must be removed from our vocabulary. Wherever the road before us might lead, faithfulness in route will bring glory to God, so we must not tarry on our departure. Time is fleeting.

During the 1986 training camp, I had the opportunity to have lunch with Joe Theismann. Joe had been an NFL MVP and Super-Bowl-winning quarterback for the Washington Redskins. On a Monday night game the previous season, a nationwide audience shuddered as they watched Lawrence Taylor sack him. Highlighted in the movie *The Blind Side*, the hit resulted in Joe suffering a compound fracture of his lower right leg which effectively ended his career.

Later that afternoon, he addressed the Notre Dame team and told them that he envied them. "Make the most of your opportunity, because most people don't get to choose when their career comes to an end." The same can be said of each of us. We do not know when an opportunity will come along the way, so we must be prepared for when our time to make a difference arrives.

Scripture tells us that the Lord determines the length of our days (Acts 17:26, Job 14:5). We do not get to choose when our time on this earth comes to a close. We only get to choose how we live today. As devoted Christian coaches, we must take the risk to reach the reward; we must escape the rut and embrace the adventure. Go there we must; go there we shall. We just need to take the first step.

2

HAVE WHAT IT TAKES!

"The One who is in you is greater than the one who is in the world."

1 John 4:4

Some coaches underestimate their influence and others don't even recognize that they have been called to coach. You might not realize it, but you and every Christ follower are coaches. No matter what you might think or how you might feel, whether or not you've ever coached before, you have all the ingredients to be a great Christian coach! Reject all the excuses and defer no longer--no negotiation or compromise. "It is not that we think we are qualified to do anything on our own. Our qualification comes from God. He has made us competent ministers of a new covenant" (2 Corinthians 3:5-6 NLT). To the Master Coach, you are a blue-chip recruit!

The Selection Process: Grafting through Drafting

Each year, a succession of student athletes will depart the collegiate ranks, either due to the expiration of their eligibility or for opportunities in the NFL, leaving some programs struggling to find their heir apparent. But not Alabama. The Crimson Tide never rebuild, they merely reload. They know exactly what they need, and they proceed to find the individual who has it all.

Fortunately, the Lord selects personnel based upon an entirely different set of criteria. As opposed to Alabama, which scours the country in search of extraordinary athletes who possess extraordinary abilities, God uses the ordinary person to do extraordinary things. You see, when that which is usually discounted becomes the preferred choice, the one who did the promoting draws the attention. Standing out from the crowd requires a strategy that avoids the status quo.

The Lord does not need us or use us based upon the abilities that we possess. The Lord's MO—method of operation—might change, but His selection process does not. To become a Christian coach, we need to possess a simple combination of ingredients: a pulse and a willing heart. They are prerequisites for team membership; attributes that enable a Christ follower to be drafted into His service and grafted into His power.

When we step out by faith to coach, we can be confident that Paul's words are true: "The one who calls you is faithful; He will do it" (1 Thessalonians 5:24). The Lord has qualified us and charged us with a commission. When we profess our faith in Jesus Christ as our Lord and Savior, not only are we qualified, but we become the newest addition to His team of coaches.

Coaching DNA: We Have All the Ingredients

Because the Holy Spirit resides in the heart of every Christ follower, there is a commonality in the composition of every Christian coach. They . . .

- Accept Ownership for Results
- Make a Long-Term Investment in Others
- Establish an Accurate Identity of Themselves
- Are Themselves Coachable, and
- Are Devoted Disciples

Ownership

Perhaps even more telling are the roles that a coach does *not* encompass. First of all, coaches are not consultants. I have often joked that I wanted to be a consultant in the NFL. As a consultant, I can express my opinion but not be responsible for the results. Consultants lack ownership--and that devalues their influence. Owners are reliable and influential because they have a stake in the matter.

A coach isn't to be a silent partner; he's to be an active participant. It's akin to Andy Stanley's phrase, "Have a ministry; don't hire a ministry." In other words, we shouldn't throw money at something. Instead, we should invest ourselves. We should be all in. The more individuals invest, the less likely they are to quit. Good coaches, like good parents, invest heavily and never stop.

> *Good coaches, like good parents, invest heavily and never stop.*

Long-Term Investment

Although coaches are not teachers, they do teach. In fact, only two letters differentiate teaching from coaching (TE and CO), and those two letters have great significance and highlight a vast separation. To me, "TE" stands for "temporary engagement," while "CO" means "continual obligation."

Coaches are more vested in their pupils' performance than most teachers. Regardless of whether the student in the classroom receives an "A" or an "F," the lecturer will still be called teacher or professor. However, in the athletic realm, if the trainers of the student athlete are unable to ensure that everyone on the team receives an "A" or a "B," they will soon be known at the school where they are presently employed as the former coach!

Christian coaches are committed to those they tutor. They don't underestimate the impact they will have on their lives, and they don't flinch in assuming these important responsibilities. Christian coaches apply a simple investment strategy: they accumulate more and more individuals to their portfolio and they never divest. By enacting this formula, they know there will be an infinite compounding on their investment and increase in the rate of their eternal return.

An Accurate Identity of Yourself

To be an effective coach, our identity must be correctly established. Unlike the periodic table of elements, which can be used to identify the ingredients in any formula, the composition of a coach cannot be so easily extracted. Our identity does not come from elements, such as our position, title, or performance. They are much too volatile for which to rely. If we look to our profession or associations for our identity, we will subject ourselves to inconsistent affirmation which will fluctuate based on our most current state. Identity based upon performance mirrors the same problems. Outcomes are often outside of our control and their buoyancy is subject to the waves of the world. This type of validation will never truly satisfy.

For some, their identity is based on exposure and experience. For instance, familiarity will generally lead them to replicate the leadership strategy under which they have been trained. They do what they know, but what do they do when that doesn't work?

In one of my earlier places of employment, I worked for a supervisor who had only served as an assistant under one person. In essence he only knew one way. Because of his lack of exposure and limited experience, he was a derivative incapable of deviation. As such, he tried his best to impersonate his lone mentor and when that failed, he attempted to impersonate others, but he never discovered his true self. Imitation may be the sincerest form of flattery, but it is not to be the foundation for our identity. It will only lead to a false impression.

In other instances, labels are sometimes incorrectly used to represent our identity. Labels help people identify but, like those that tag articles of clothing, they are poor interpreters of who we are. They usher in generalizations that overlook the uniqueness of each individual and for this reason they have limited worth. Labels refer to a person's roles, responsibilities, associations, race, gender, birth origin, and a host of other characteristics.

Although we have a natural tendency to classify, even going so far as to classify ourselves, we must remember that these labels are, at best, an oversimplification and, at worst, detrimental. Some of these personal summaries are harmless, while others are impactful, leading to some of the most constructive or destructive perceptions one might have of oneself. Not only does the description we ascribe to ourselves affect our self-image, the label can also alter the lens in which we see our world. If we feel good about ourselves, we tend to feel good about those around us. However, if we have a poor self-image, it decreases the likelihood that our interactions will be productive. These labels do not, and cannot, accurately and completely reflect who we are, so they can't serve as the basis of our identity.

Coaches must be correctly identified as it is a foundational element that will largely impact their coaching success. Practically speaking, this means that coaches should be careful when assigning themselves a label and hesitant when it comes to creating one for others, for there is always one far more qualified for such a task.

In 2014, when Sean and Rikki McEvoy strolled into a Goodwill store in Asheville, North Carolina, little did they know that a ragged old item they would purchase would actually become a worthwhile investment. The object that caught their attention that day was a sweater with the West Point logo on the front which was hung on one of the clearance racks. It had a tear but, as the saying goes, "one man's junk is another man's treasure," so they bought the item and returned home.

It wasn't until they watched a documentary on television the next year, that they wondered if there was an association with the seemingly worthless garment and the person featured on the telecast. When they looked at the name that was stitched on a tag inside the sweater, they realized that it indeed might be a personal artifact that once belonged to this historic individual. The Heritage Auction House of Dallas, Texas, confirmed the authenticity by analyzing the material, and the method of stitching that composed this unique piece of clothing. The letter sweater was once the property of the legendary coach for whom the Super Bowl trophy is named: Vince Lombardi. The McEvoy's spent $0.58 in the thrift store that day, but when the sweater was auctioned one year later, it sold for $43,020. They made nearly 75,000 times what they initially spent![1] The value was not ascribed to the sweater; its value was in for whom it was made.

Our value exists because we were made for the Heavenly Father. He is the owner and we are a collectible of infinite worth because we were purchased at a high price: the sacrifice of God's lone Son (John 3:16). He is the only one allowed to label us. Our label is that of a Christ follower, and He has identified and made each one of us unique. If our identities are not grounded in Christ, we are sure to have an identity crisis and, if it remains uncorrected, we will only continue to perpetuate a lie. Any classification, based on anything other than the Word of God and a personal relationship with His Son, will be founded on an imperfect model and an incomplete basis of knowledge.

Once again, if the way we view ourselves is skewed, then everything external will be compromised as well. We need to look upward for our identity, not outward or even inward. The same is true even if people have already identified you as a coach. At the press conference that announced my retirement from coaching college football, I stated that coaching football is what I do; it is not who I am. My title and profession have changed, but not my identity. My identity remains constant, consistent, and independent of my endeavors. Our identity must not come from what we do, but for whom we are created and for the reason of our existence. Ownership and role should define our identity. We belong to our Savior, and we were designed to coach.

Coaches are Coachable

C. S. Lewis wisely wrote, "Experience is a brutal teacher. But you'll learn, by God, you'll learn."

Task Switching

Coaches learn on the job. We constantly funnel what we learn into demonstration. The objective of our education is to impart what we know to those we coach. We can learn multiple lessons at one time, but we cannot perform multiple tasks concurrently. It is just part of our makeup. Good coaches don't multitask, they task switch.

Task switching involves the efficient shift from one task undertaking to another. Whereas multitasking can contribute to poor performance, task switching directs attention to one matter at a time so as to channel all our energies to that which we prioritized. One example in which the coach might task switch is from the role of teacher to that of student. It's a dual role. We are always transforming while transporting. As such, coaches themselves must remain coachable—teaching while being taught. From student to trainer and back again, the switch is so subtle and indiscernible that it appears to happen simultaneously.

> *We are always transforming while transporting. As such, coaches themselves must remain coachable—teaching while being taught.*

Devoted Disciples

"It's not what you know, but what they know that counts" and a coach understands that both are crucial. Coaches never stop learning. To be a good learner, we must keep at it; we must remain a disciple of the Master Teacher. The word disciple is derived from the term discipline. It means steadfast or one who is truly devoted. What is considered important is reinforced for emphasis and, to illustrate just how important it is that we continue in Christ, the word disciple is repeated over 260 times in the gospels and in the Book of Acts!

In the Bible, disciple also meant learner. In Greek, the term for learned, *manthano*, and for disciple, *mathetes*, are closely related. Biblical theologian Warren Wiersbe, affectionately known as "the pastor's pastor," says that does not denote a halfhearted effort, but "a total surrender to the teaching. It meant learning by living." Coaches are lifelong learners, because they are lifelong disciples.

C.O.A.C.H. Stands for Something!

Acronyms simplify by building a word from more extensive components. The newly formed word replaces lengthy sentences that describe a process, area, organization, and a host of other possibilities. Succeeding chapters will elaborate on each component, but for now, Christian coaches possess five ingredients. They are...

- **Commissioned:** They have been charged with a purpose and calling that originated from above.
- **Owners:** They take responsibility for outcomes and the means used to achieve those outcomes.
- **Assemblers:** They bring together the people and processes to initiate change.
- **Committed:** They are devoted to the Lord and dedicated to finishing what they began.
- **Helpmates:** They assist others in their pursuit of spiritual objectives.

3

CHANGE THE GAME

"A coach remains something or someone that takes a valued person from where they are to where they want to be."

Kevin Hall

Kevin Hall's definition of a coach is a definition of leadership; it involves the transfer of people and a vehicle of delivery. Many articles and books have been written about the various forms of leadership. They range in terms of control from one who is laissez-faire (almost exclusively hands-off), to the micromanager (a person who is nearly entirely hands-on). One soars at the 30,000-foot level; the other is constantly down in the weeds, and there is a variety of leadership approaches between these two ends of the continuum.

Some are defined by personal characteristics, such as charisma, while others are identified by their situation and style—such as innovative and transformational. But there is one form that transcends style, situation, and control, one model of leadership that is multifunctional and stands out from the rest—the leadership of a coach. Regardless of the situation, figuratively or literally, coaching is the leadership approach that will best guide the valued person (VP) "from where they are to where they want to be." Like pioneers leading a wagon train, coaches "head 'em up, and move 'em out!"

Coaches Pave the Way

Coaches are modern-day explorers enthusiastically setting out on their next adventure. Explorers find passages to carry themselves and their precious cargo safely along a new trail to a new frontier. Pioneers such as Magellan, Lewis and Clark, and John Glenn discovered previously unknown corridors that would map the route for generations to follow. Whether navigating the high seas, crossing new terrain, or reaching for the stars, their efforts made what was once considered implausible possible, and the exceptionally difficult, routine.

Unstable times and uncharted courses call for unconventional methods and uncommon leadership. Like the good explorer, the coach must lead new disciples on the only road that matters, and Jesus, the ultimate trailblazer, explains how: "Enter through the narrow gate. For wide is the gate and broad is the road that leads to destruction, and many enter through it. But small is the gate and narrow is the road that leads to life, and only a few find it" (Matthew 7:13-14).

> *Unstable times and uncharted courses call for unconventional methods and uncommon leadership.*

It matters what route we take since only one ensures we will reach our heavenly home. Jesus left no room for doubt when He told His disciples, "I am the way and the truth and the life. No one comes to the Father except through me" (John 14:6). The roadmap is quite simple: there is only one highway to heaven. As Christ followers, we are the few who have found the Way, but we are not to travel unaccompanied.

It is our responsibility to help others find their way there as well. Coaches don't just lead, they deliver.

What Drives the Driver

According to the *Cambridge Dictionary*, gumption is "the ability to decide what is the best thing to do in a particular situation, and to do it with energy and determination."

Action is vital to a vibrant life. We see a special suffix "tion" that forms nouns that express action. What drives the coach drives the process. For coaches, our movement should be expressed by our motivation, inspiration, aspiration, and perspiration. Our motivation is that we don't know how long we have. Our inspiration is the people we have an opportunity to influence. Our aspiration is to display Christ to them. And perspiration is what will be required to accomplish the task.

There is much work for us to accomplish as we travel this road. Our role is an active, not a passive one because the consequences are everlasting. When it comes to what needs to be done, coaches have gumption; they don't shun; they "tion."

> *When it comes to what needs to be done, coaches have gumption; they don't shun; they "tion."*

Coaching Classifications

Coaching is a noble profession, but in recent years there has been a negative stigma attached to its name. The poor behavior of a few bad actors has tainted the good reputation of the rest. Despite the few exceptions, the word "coach," far and away, has a positive connotation. If it didn't, the term would not be used so frequently and in so many contexts, and its popularity continues to rise. Although the term can be attached to practically any endeavor, I believe that the pervasive use of the jargon can be narrowed into four specific categories:

1. Athletic
2. Personal or Life
3. Professional
4. Spiritual

The most common reference to coaching relates, of course, to the athletic realm, but the title of the coach has become increasingly popular in other fields. Personal (or Life) Coaches seek to enhance the quality of each person's existence, while Professional Coaches serve to advance their clients toward the achievement of career goals. Finally, Spiritual Coaches look to give meaning to life and perspective to the afterlife. There is a common thread that links all four classifications. The coach is a tenured position, a treasured relationship, and a trusted guide whose sole purpose is to deliver the goods.

The importance of our role as coaches should never be underestimated. Billy Graham once said, "A coach will have more impact in one year than an average person will in a lifetime." Coaches have an awesome responsibility and an incredible opportunity to impact those around them. Coaching is a leadership skill set that can be incorporated into all our capacities, but we do it a disservice if we describe it as just another means of influence. It is more than influence. It's been said that leaders influence, and that is simply not true. Everyone influences; the key is whether it will be positive or negative influence that is imparted. The Bible reminds us that it is for this reason that associations matter: "Do not be misled: 'Bad company corrupts good character'" (1 Corinthians 15:33).

This is one of the reasons why we all need to join a "coaches association" (church). Our membership links us, both spiritually and relationally, with other like-minded individuals and reinforces the coaching doctrine to which we subscribe. It might be true that "birds of a feather flock together," but it can also be said that "birds who flock together morph into birds of a feather." Rarely does anyone get into trouble alone. If we gravitate to the wrong people, it won't just be gravity that will be pulling us down, and when someone goes down they almost always take someone with them.

Recently, a pastor friend shared a story that supports this theory. In a late inning of his daughter's softball game, the opposing coach inserted a relief pitcher. However, the girl that he sent to the mound had arrived at the ballpark well past the deadline that league rules stipulated for participation in a game. Although the coach was well aware of the rules, he broke them anyway. When the umpire confronted the coach and informed him that his athlete would not be allowed to play, instead of replacing her, the coach decided to forfeit the game! He reasoned that, since they were behind and the likelihood of them winning was a low probability, he would rather just end the game. On the ball diamond, as in life, sometimes we learn how to and sometimes we learn how not to.

Unfortunately, when presented with teachable moments for the pupils on his squad, the coach taught them lessons in the latter. First, by knowingly making an illegal substitution, the coach endorsed cheating (or at least a "win-at-all-costs" mentality). Second, by forfeiting the game, the coach introduced quitting as a viable option. Third, the lack of sportsmanship he displayed not only abbreviated the contest; it negated the opportunity for the young ladies on both squads to continue developing their softball skills. By doing these things, the coach took an entire team down with him. My prayer is that the parents were able to counter the negative influence their children received that day.

Conversely, leaders also can exert a positive influence on a group. As Hall of Fame football coach Vince Lombardi once pointed out, "The strength of the group is the strength of the leaders," and, as disciples of Jesus Christ, we are leaders who are able to tap into an omnipotent strength. "You don't need a telescope, a microscope, or a horoscope to realize the fullness of Christ, and the emptiness of the universe without him. When you come to him, that fullness comes together for you, too. His power extends over everything" (Colossians 2:9-10 MSG).

He is the supplement that enriches our composition. We should not discount what we can achieve, because He is the ceaseless source of energy from which we coaches can draw. As coaches, we have the power to positively impact everyone within our reach. If we are observant, within our sphere of influence, a host of opportunities awaits.

Ironically, we do not have the luxury of passively sitting by with the intent of not affecting the world around us. As Christ said, "Whoever is not with me is against me" (Matthew 12:30). There is a line that is drawn and no one can remain neutral. When it comes to coaching, there are no conscientious objectors.

If we ascertain that we will be content living a reclusive life and that our seclusion will not impact others, we are sadly mistaken. Our influence can occur unwittingly or intentionally, but regardless of how it happens, its aftereffect can extend beyond our ability to comprehend. Countless numbers of people, over centuries, can be shaped by our actions in both monumental and less impressive ways. While some events can seem minute and of little consequence at the time, myriads of examples exist of a person influencing his peers in a seemingly innocent manner, only to later realize that they cast a lasting impression on the world.

On a Mission from God

Life is full of breaking and junction points. In the game of football, a breaking point occurs when a wide receiver alters the course of his route. Shortly thereafter, that action is usually followed with an intersecting junction point where the football thrown from the quarterback is intended to reach the receiver's hands.

For a Christian coach, a breaking point occurs when we realize our mission and redirect our route to fulfill it. A junction point takes place when our leadership intersects with the journey of a valuable person. On the football field, as in life, it is all about being at the right place at the right time.

At pivotal junctures—and especially perilous times—people will look to you for leadership, just as they have always looked to those God has appointed. A breaking point can occur anywhere and at any time. One moment you might feel like you are aimlessly traveling about, and then in an instant, you realize what must be done, and that you are the person who can best provide the junction between the VP and the next step toward their divine destiny.

Joshua was the designated "head coach" during a climactic time in Jewish history. In stereotypical coaching fashion, Joshua gave the order that transported an entire civilization from the land where they wandered to the land for which they longed, and he employed a coaching staff to ensure his game plan was enacted: "When you see the ark of the covenant of the Lord your God, and the Levitical priests carrying it, you are to move out from your positions and follow it" (Joshua 3:3).

There is an unmistakable parallel between the priests of old and the Christ follower of today. The priests carried the ark, and in so doing, transported the Lord across the Jordan River and into the Promised Land. As believers, we are now the ones who assume that awesome responsibility. Since the Holy Spirit resides within us, we are the "coaches" who carry our Lord, so we must make every step count. As we go where He leads (breaking points), like the priests who crossed the riverbed ahead of the Israelite nation, others are sure to follow (junction points). Transporting begins with God and ends with the VP and the coach each moving closer to where the Lord wants them to be.

It's not about our position; it's about His presence and power. "But for this purpose I have raised you up," says the Lord, "to show you my power, so that my name may be proclaimed in all the earth" (Exodus 9:16 ESV). Your position may not be elevated to the level of Joshua, but it has been assigned from above. Regardless of your rank, your position is vital as well.

In the words of Joliet Jake and Elwood Blues (from the 1980s smash hit *The Blues Brothers*), truly you "are on a mission from God."

4

HAVE A PURPOSE AND CALLING

"He has saved us and called us to a holy life—not because of anything we have done but because of His own purpose and grace."

2 Timothy 1:9

We all wear a lot of hats: husbands and wives, mothers and fathers, grandfathers and grandmothers, brothers and sisters, and sons and daughters. Professionally, our responsibilities are as varied as our occupations are numerous, but life is not about a title we have assumed or a position we hold. There is a common ground that transcends our many roles and a primary function for all we do—our lives are about purpose and calling. Every believer has a "good purpose" (Philippians 2:13) and a "holy calling" (2 Timothy 1:9). Keep in mind that our job descriptions are specific to us and come with a promise that there will be "additional duties as assigned." Our title, role, or position can change but, like our identity, our purpose and calling remain constant.

For instance, in football, the purpose of the offensive unit is twofold: score or kick it away. Any other alternative (fumble, interception, or safety) has a negative outcome. Regardless of their offensive position (i.e. quarterback or offensive lineman), the purpose stays the same. As Christ followers, John Piper says, "the Bible is crystal clear: God created us for His glory," and this purpose is not open to debate. It is the underlying premise in everything we do.

Whatever You Do

"Whatever you do, work at it with all your heart, as working for the Lord, not for man... It is the Lord you are serving" (Colossians 3:23-24 NIV '84).

The passage not only reinforces that it is the Lord for whom we work, but it expounds upon that idea. "Whatever you do" translates to anything, anywhere, at any time. "With all your heart" means the Lord expects our finest work. "Not for man" is not dismissive of the responsibility we have to serve others. Our efforts should always improve the quality of life and interaction with our fellow man. The "not for man" statement supports the notion that it is the Lord whom we serve and should desire to please. "Whatever you do" is a phrase that demands full integration into every aspect of our lives, and a command from which we must not retreat. When addressing the church in Corinth, Paul doubles down on the point by using the same three words again: "So whether you eat or drink or whatever you do, do it all for the glory of God" (1 Corinthians 10:31).

Paul's assertion is that our purpose in life is to bring glory to God. It is all-inclusive and at the focal point of our existence.

Lastly, in 1 Peter, we learn that we are to use our spiritual gifts so that everything we "do will bring glory to God through Jesus Christ" (4:11). It is impossible to please God through any other means but Christ. Our purpose unites us with Christ's work at Calvary and with one another. It has existed from the beginning and will continue forever more—whatever we do.

A Transformation Model

Christian coaches can now explore the manner in which purpose may be accomplished. The only way to achieve our role on earth is through our transformation into the likeness of Jesus Christ. We are to mirror Christ and, in so doing, we will reflect His character in our conduct. As Christ followers, we should emulate, rather than imitate, Jesus' example; this is a subtle, but important distinction. Imitation mimics what is original. It can be a "knockoff" or a nearly flawless reproduction. We emulate the Son of Man, not methodology.

I experienced this firsthand. I turned down paid coaching positions in order to remain a graduate assistant at Notre Dame, not because of the institution, and not because of the offensive and defensive schemes that the new coaching staff would employ. I chose to stay because of Lou Holtz. For me, it was about following a man, not a pattern. I had the utmost respect for Coach Holtz—and I still do. Professionally, he could take me places I could not have otherwise gone. I am where I am today, in large part, because he helped transport me there.

I follow Jesus Christ for the same reason—He takes me places I cannot go on my own. I know it is about following the Son of Man, not imitating His methods. My goal is to transform into His image, not learn a system. Professionally, I had been mentored by a master coach; personally, I continue to be mentored by the Master Coach. My intention is to do my part to mentor others, thus transporting these VPs "from where they are to where they want to be." Christian coaches are called to become less like ourselves and more like Him. Our transformational terminus is the emulation of Christ. When people look at us, what will they see? If they emulate us, what will they look like?

Our mission in life is not linked to a profession, title, possession, or any other causes of the world; it's about our transformation. Believers are, as Peter said, "living stones being built up as a spiritual house" (1 Peter 2:5 ESV). Individually, story upon story, like a superintendent of a construction site, Jesus will take every Christian coach from ground-level to an ever-perpetuating succession of new elevations until our spiritual house is completed. As we develop, we appreciate opportunities to live out our goal and receive eternal rewards for our faithfulness.

Purpose: A Transformation Model
"The Construction of a Coach"

Our purpose has been around since antiquity and will never change. Remember, you are not in this alone. Christian coaches exist interdependently and independently of one another. Coaches are interdependent because we share the same purpose, and we are independent in the manner in which we accomplish our purpose. And that is true for our calling as well.

Calling

Calling undergirds purpose. *Vocatio* is the Latin word for calling. Although it is the root for vocation, a calling is not a job, nor is it a career. A job has a finite existence and an individual can have more than one career (I'm living proof of this fact). A calling transcends time; it can be developed and transferred. Calling points to a greater meaning and refers to the way we apply our purpose.

In *Grit*, Angela Duckworth provides an illustration that serves to better understand the meaning of a calling:

The Parable of the Bricklayers

Three bricklayers were asked, "What are you doing?" The first one says, "I am laying bricks." The second says, "I am building a church." And the third says, "I am building the house of God." The first bricklayer has a job. The second has a career. The third has a calling.[1]

On the subject of calling, Oswald Chambers once said, "A person realizes their calling from God with a sudden thunderclap or with a gradual dawning, but in whatever way it comes, it comes with an undercurrent of the supernatural, something that cannot be put into words." In the physical world, mirrors are props that can be helpful in illustrating calling. Mirrors have multiple purposes in which they can be applied. Mirrors not only reflect, but they also deflect light. Our job is to reflect the image of Christ and, simultaneously, redirect the Light of the World, Jesus Christ, on to others. Our calling is to take other people with us; our calling is to coach.

A Transportation Model

In the production of a new coach, the veteran coach leads his or her VP on a course that includes four key steps: Engage, Escort, Equip, and Empower. It is a mutually beneficial progression. As coaches direct others through the faith-training process—as they Engage, Escort, Equip, and Empower—they themselves continue to develop spiritually alongside those they have been called to transport. We are to transmit the Truth and then continue to transport the VP; to disciple them toward ever-increasing levels of spiritual maturity.

As those we guide transform into the likeness of Jesus Christ, they themselves will become coaches equipped to transport valued persons within the context of their lives. Christian coaches equip themselves so that they can initiate a training process in the VP. As we undergo metamorphosis, we inspire the same alteration in those we lead. The end of the journey is the creation of a disciple, a new member of the coaching fraternity.

Calling: A Transportation Model
"The Production of a Disciple"

Coach/VP ⟶ Engage ⟶ Escort ⟶ Equip ⟶ Empower ⟶ New Coach

Christian coaches not only partner with the VP, we need to comprehend that we are in a partnership with God. The torch has been passed to this generation of Christian coaches. We have been tasked with the duty of providing for the welfare of others; it is something we should not trivialize. We have been endowed by our Creator with many gifts and He doesn't mince words when He says that "from everyone who has been given much, much will be demanded; and from the one who has been entrusted with much, much more will be asked" (Luke 12:48). Our charge is to not violate that trust.

Our God has established a clearly defined division of duties. Our job is to faithfully execute our calling—the results are up to Him. All we must do is be willing to be used by God and then boldly coach the people He puts on our path.

Leadership expert Brad Lomenick says, "Without courage, your calling is crippled. Even if you have a crystal-clear vision from God about the path you should pursue—and most of us don't—it will not alter your direction one whit until you have enough courage to act upon it. Courage moves us from ideals to action, from potential to actuality."

5

FIND YOUR ZONE— AND STAY IN IT

"For God has put it into their hearts to accomplish His purpose..."

Revelation 17:17

While calling refers to the application of our purpose, context pertains to the demographics that are specific to each individual. God gives each Christian coach a context within which to fulfill their calling. At home, at work, and all points in between, each coach has a context designed exclusively for them that will allow them influence in certain spheres.

While our context will change over time, our calling spans the duration of our lives. It's not over until we cross over! We are

If you're breathing, there's a reason; there's still work to do.

never too old to start or start over. You are never too old to add significance to someone's life. If you're breathing, there's a reason; there's still work to do. Jesus breathed life into us through the Holy Spirit. As long as the Spirit moves in us, we are to move in the lives of others. God's faithful coaches never retire.

Conversely, although federal regulation prohibits employment to those who are underage, we are never too young to begin a coaching career. In instructing Timothy, Paul reminds every youthful disciple, "Don't let anyone think less of you because you are young. Be an example to all believers in what you say, in the way you live, in your love, your faith, and your purity" (1 Timothy 4:12 NLT).

Former University of Colorado Head Football Coach Bill McCartney can attest to the power of influence that can be imparted by youthful Christ followers. In his book, *From Ashes to Glory*[1], the coach who would lead the Buffaloes to the 1990 national championship testifies that Chuck Heater was instrumental in his decision to surrender his life to Jesus Christ. As a defensive back at the University of Michigan (where McCartney then served as the defensive coordinator), Heater's consistent example drew the attention of this future Hall of Fame coach. In this instance, the player was the coach, and the coach was the VP.

Not only did Coach McCartney establish a very successful collegiate coaching career, he went on to create Promise Keepers (an international Christ-centered organization dedicated to the spiritual growth of men). Since its founding in 1990, this nonprofit evangelical ministry has grown from an initial gathering of seventy-two individuals to stadium-filled conferences attended by the tens of thousands. Over its thirty-plus years in existence, the number of men who have benefited from this parachurch organization is countless. And, it all began when one observant coach was drawn to the unique behavior of one student athlete.

Similarly, Jesus began His ministry by calling twelve unqualified men to join His team. To many, they lacked the skills, training, and the influence to accomplish anything that would make a meaningful contribution. In addition, they were also too young. A number of biblical scholars contend that, with the exception of Peter, the apostles were all teenagers.

Jesus' staff was comprised of four fisherman, one tax collector, and seven whose means of livelihood is still unknown. All were considered "second-class" individuals, as they had been rejected for the advanced study that was required for them to become rabbis (a position of status and the preferred role of every Jewish boy in that time period). Yet it is amazing what God can do through people who possess the wrong pedigree. It's not a matter of age, education, or any other demographic; it's a matter of the heart. Eleven boys became devoted disciples who would follow Him to the end, and through the actions of these "unqualified" coaches, the world has never been the same.

Passions

Passions, like context, provide avenues for connection with VPs. Passions are interests that can manifest themselves in hobbies, careers, or recreational pursuits. Basically, every tangible and intangible aspect of your life provides a context or a passion that allows you to develop relationships. They are the instruments the Lord has choreographed to strategically spread the Good News of salvation through Jesus Christ for the redemption of the world.

Although they may not realize it, Harvard University employs this biblical principle in their admission process for undergraduates. Contrary to popular opinion, the university does not look exclusively at those who might academically be considered "elite" candidates. The widely held belief that only rich kids go to Harvard is also a fallacy. Harvard takes great pride in the fact that they have been integral in promoting the advancement of those who come from the middle and lower economic classes.

Our 1997 Ivy League championship team is representative of this philosophy. Of our twenty-four starters on that squad, twenty-two of them received financial assistance based on economic need. While high academic marks are certainly a prerequisite, and children of alumni ("legacies") are given special consideration, the attractive characteristics they designate are much more extensive.

As part of the preenrollment procedure, Harvard requires each applicant to consent to a personal interview. There are two reasons for the mandatory meeting. First, Harvard believes that 50 percent of the education that the students receive comes from the classroom and 50 percent is derived through the interaction they have with the student body. Everything that makes an applicant unique also makes them attractive to admissions officers and a partner in the university's quest to provide a comprehensive education. In short, entry to the university is dependent upon a strategy that incorporates context and passions. Whether a person is from a rural or metropolitan area, a US citizen or international student, a host of other criteria are factored into their contextual assessment. At all times, Harvard wants a cross-section of the world present on its campus.

Passions are equally attractive to the institution. Very few people realize that, at this world-renowned mecca of higher education, the athletic department boasts the largest number of sports programs in the United States. Nearly one in four undergraduates admitted to the university compete on one of their forty-two intercollegiate teams. During my tenure on the football staff, the Harvard Crimson athletic department was comprised of more student athletes than the combined total of any other two major universities.

The second reason for the personal interview of its applicants is to determine whether they are capable of conveying their context and passions to others. As a Christ follower, if we are unwilling to use that which we have been

given in service to the
Lord, like an applicant for
Harvard University who is
unwilling—or incapable—
of expressing themselves,
we have limited value.

*Passion is not the same
thing as our purpose; it is
the means to an end, not the
end itself.*

Passion is not the same thing as our purpose; it is the means
to an end, not the end itself. Our passions must align with
our purpose, but never should our passion become mistaken
for our purpose. Many a man has set a course incorrectly and
misguidedly pursued their passion as if it were their primary
mission in life. Purpose should always take precedence over
passion.

Passions present platforms, and platforms provide
opportunities for us to serve or speak, on behalf of the Lord.
Professional trade associations, local service organizations
such as Rotary Clubs, and personal affiliations based on
hobbies and interests (i.e. book clubs and the PTA) form the
basis for collectively pursuing passions. All are indicative of
opportunities in which we might be able to maximize our
advantage.

On more than one occasion, Tim Tebow has leveraged his
love for athletics as an avenue to promote his faith. When he
wrote "John 3:16" on his eye black prior to the 2009 national
championship game, the initiative prompted 94 million
people to google the well-known Scripture verse! Three
years to the day later, Tim Tebow led the Denver Broncos
to an upset overtime playoff victory over the Pittsburgh
Steelers, which set up an AFC Championship game versus
the New England Patriots. Amazingly, on the anniversary
of the "John 3:16 game," he threw for 316 yards, 31.6 yards
per completion, his rushing yards per attempt were 3.16,
the TV ratings for the contest were 31.6, and the Broncos'
time of possession was 31.06! Oh yeah, one thing more:
during the game, an additional 91 million people googled

John 3:16. Once again, the verse became the top trending item on every social platform.[2] (By the way, I don't believe in coincidences. I advocate what I heard somebody once say: "A coincidence is a small miracle for which God chooses to remain anonymous.")

You don't have to play football and you do not have to be Tim Tebow to make an impact. Whether you perform on a national stage or the equivalent of a local playhouse, every Christian coach is afforded occasions for engagement. To accomplish our calling to take people with us and realize our purpose of glorifying God, while becoming more and more like His Son, we must leverage our context and passions.

Once again, like context, over time some interests may wane and new ones appear, but our calling and purpose will remain unaltered. As the driver, we must stay engaged with the VP to deliver us both to the destination.

6

HAVE A GAME PLAN

*"It's not the will to win that matters—everyone has that.
It's the will to prepare to win that matters."*
                                        Paul "Bear" Bryant

Coaches don't "wing it." They game plan. So much so that football truly is a game of inches! If an athletic contest can come down to something so small, then how much more attention should we Christian coaches pay on our journey and to the pathway of those we have been called to lead? Surely, the outcome of life is greater than the outcome of the game.

Mission Statements and Constitutions

Government and business entities have created constitutions and mission statements to clearly convey the purpose of their existence to their constituents. If audibly and visibly referenced enough, this game plan will become innate in the individuals that comprise their organization, will effectively govern their actions, and will increase the probability of achieving their goals. Christian coaches optimize their desired outcomes when they follow suit.

The Fellowship of Christian Athletes (FCA) is a parachurch organization that has been a part of my family's life for over fifty years. Its mission statement reads as follows:

> To present to coaches and athletes, and all whom they influence, the challenge and adventure of receiving Jesus Christ as Savior and Lord, serving Him in their relationships and in the fellowship of the church.[1]

Their mission statement includes purpose, calling, context, and passion. Their purpose is to lead others to Christ and into the community of a local church. Their calling is to take people with them. Their context is implicit in that they influence student athletes of all ages. Finally, their passion is athletics.

Like flour mixing in dough, personal mission statements knead together our purpose with the other ingredients of calling, context, and passion—our hope is that they become baked into our very being.

Your Personal Mission Statement

In Romans, Paul gives his personal mission statement: "It has always been my ambition to preach the gospel where Christ was not known, so that I would not be building on someone else's foundation. Rather, as it is written: 'Those who were not told about Him will see, and those who have not heard will understand'" (15:20-21).

Paul's purpose was to bring glory to God by proclaiming salvation through Jesus Christ. He was called to transport Gentiles—those who were not kosher Jews—into a relationship with the promised Messiah. He incorporated his passion to preach the gospel to those who have previously not heard it. Clearly, Paul was a premier coach of his time—of all time! Paul had a game plan that helped ensure that he remained focused on the task he was assigned. Like Paul, our personal mission statement acts as a game plan that keeps us pointed in the right direction.

Formerly an agnostic, Nancy Pearcey has become a premier evangelistic author and decorated scholar. She states, "The biblical message is not just about some isolated part of life labeled 'religion' or 'church life.' The promise of Christianity is the joy and power of an integrated life, transformed on every level by the Holy Spirit, so that our whole being participates in the great drama of God's plan of redemption."[2]

It is impossible live without presuppositions that form the basis of our worldview. Either we will have a secular mindset or a biblical worldview that will permeate all our interactions. Our game plan is not for isolated use on Sunday morning; it should pervade every waking moment. At home, work, and in the community, Christian coaches must carry out their game plan every day of the week.

A Family Mission Statement

Families provide a setting for some of the most important roles we assume, that of a son or daughter, mother or father. Constitutions are to the family what mission statements are to the individual. They are game plans intended to give the family purpose, direction, and unity as they live life together. Since more than one person is asked to submit to the constitution, it is imperative that each family member has a voice in its creation. In this manner, ownership is enhanced and its contents are more likely to be adopted.

As Christian coaches, applying biblically based coaching principles begins at home. As parents, our responsibility is to impress God's Word upon our children, and our game plan is found in the Old Testament. Deuteronomy is clear about this responsibility commanding that parents and guardians must "commit [themselves] wholeheartedly to these words of mine" (11:18).

Scripture goes on to admonish parents to "teach them to your children. Talk about them when you are at home and when you are on the road, when you are going to bed, and when you are getting up. Write them on the doorposts of your house and on your gates, so that as long as the sky remains above the earth, you and your children may flourish" (11:19-21 NLT).

Children and youth are the most important VPs we are called to coach and whose lives we will lead.

The family constitution was intended to not only govern our lives together, but also be a document that would bridge them to independence and adulthood. The rule presented in Proverbs 22:6 is familiar to many parents: "Train up a child in the way they should go and when they are old they will not turn from it." It's another biblical principle that works.

Although my children are now grown and out of the home, my hope is that they have internalized the Mills Family Constitution so that it still remains a vibrant part of their lives, and through them, they might strike a chord with the next generation. Appendix A contains the Mills Family Constitution. It was created years ago as we sat together at our kitchen table. I trust it can be useful as a blueprint as you and your family create your own.

Personal mission statements and family constitutions should be reviewed frequently. In order for coaches to keep first things first, we must ingrain our purpose and calling into our long-term memory. Recording our game plan on paper increases the likelihood that we will not deviate from what we set out to do. There is something impactful about putting something in writing. And so, during one of the most challenging times of my life, I made it a routine to review my personal mission statement daily.

Write It Down

For one year, I shadowed Coach Holtz and either wrote down every word that he uttered or captured it on a microcassette recorder. If he turned around too quickly, he was apt to trip over me! There is no question that the knowledge I obtained from this experience was parlayed into successes I would later enjoy in my coaching career. And I still use the lessons learned from him today. Lessons that are not written down are highly unlikely to be remembered, let alone become integrated into our routine or transferred to others.

In 1979, Harvard University studied MBA graduates to determine how goal setting might impact achievement. The class was asked one question: Have you written goals and created a plan for their attainment? Only 13 percent of the graduates had written goals while another 3 percent of the class had concrete plans in addition to written goals. Ten years later, an analysis of the graduating class found that the 13 percent of the students who had written goals had incomes twice that of the 84 percent that did not set goals. But, here's the statistic that's especially interesting: the 3 percent of the graduates that had both written and set plans were making ten times more money than the other 97 percent of their classmates.[3]

As a coach, I incorporated this principle without exception. Each year, after consulting with our Players Council, our team's mission was printed on a banner that would be displayed in a location to serve as a daily reminder to each team member. In addition, before it was hung, every coach and squad member signed their name to our mission statement. In this way, it acted as a covenant and, as has already been stated, when we write things down—especially, when the thing we transcribe is our name—our objective is more likely to be accomplished.

In summary, our game plan weaves together the components of purpose, calling, context, and passion into a personal mission statement. It is a living document that prepares us as coaches for our discipleship journey, reminds us of our role in His plan, and directs us to the people we are to coach. It is incorporated as we kick off our ministry, remains active until the gun sounds to conclude our game of life, and is integrated in all that we do in the interval between. Executing the game plan is a matter of vision and priority.

Focus: A Function of Priority

A Christian coach needs a game plan to make the most of every moment. It is too important to be left to chance. Without a game plan, an opportunity of a lifetime might pass us by. In his book *The Grave Robber*, Mark Batterson provides a frame of reference:

> On a January morning in 2007, a world-class violinist played six of Johann Sebastian Bach's most stirring solo concertos on a 300-year-old Stradivarius worth $3.5 million. Two nights before, Joshua Bell had performed a sold-out concert where patrons gladly paid $200 for nosebleed seats, but this time the performance was free.
>
> Bell ditched his tux with coattails, donned a Washington Nationals baseball cap, and played incognito outside of the L'Enfant Plaza Metro station. Street musicians are not an uncommon sight or sound for Washingtonians.
>
> The experiment was originally conceived by *Washington Post* columnist Gene Weingarten and filmed by hidden camera. Of the 1,097 people who passed by, only seven stopped to listen. The forty-

five-minute performance ended without applause or acknowledgment. Joshua Bell netted $32.17 in tips, which included a $20 spot from the one person who recognized the Grammy Award–winning musician.

On an average workday nearly a million passengers ride Washington's Metro system, and L'Enfant Plaza is one of the busiest stops. A stampede of tourists and government employees hustle and bustle through the turnstiles, trying to get where they're going as quickly as possible. But those circumstances don't discredit or disqualify the question raised by the social experiment: If we do not have a moment to stop and listen to one of the greatest musicians in the world, playing some of the finest music ever written, on one of the most beautiful instruments ever made, how many similarly sublime moments do we miss out on during a normal day? [4]

"You can't miss it!" At one time or another, each of us have been on the receiving end of that message. These four words make me cringe each time they are spoken. To me, the one who utters this cliché adds unwarranted pressure to its recipient. Implicitly, what's being said is that you must be a complete idiot if you don't see it. But I've missed it and a lot of others have missed seeing it as well.

When we "miss it" it is typically because we're looking in the wrong direction, we've misunderstood the instructions, or we've been distracted by our circumstances. In all three instances, the common denominator is that we were not paying attention.

In 1998, psychologists Arien Mack and Irvin Rock coined the term "inattentional blindness" in their book by the same name. [5] Also referenced by Batterson, their study showed that people often fail to perceive even very major things that are occurring right in front of their eyes. Perception is primarily a matter of attentiveness, and attentiveness is mainly a function of priority.

During the athletic recruiting process, coaches present the many appealing aspects that their university affords the prospect. Some of their selling points feature items of great substance, while other characteristics, although they are appealing, are details that are much less significant. The latter should really be classified as non-factors. However, I have encountered many young men who became so enamored with the bells and whistles that were presented that they lost sight of the things they initially set out to attain. Unless they were able to separate the garnish from the main course, they were apt to sign with a university and later find out that their choice did not satisfy their appetite. The result? A number of them would flounder—academically as well as athletically—and many would look to transfer. In short, they missed it, and they are not alone.

Some will have missed it as they invested their lives in the pursuit of worldly wealth, acquisition, and power. Still, well-intentioned others, who attempt to find their purpose in life, have invested in noble causes. They had a vision and a way to keep it.

Not too long ago, my wife and I returned from visiting a couple of our sons in Seattle. While there, we spent part of one day perusing the Bill and Melinda Gates Foundation Visitors Center. Besides co-founding Microsoft—what would become the world's largest PC software company—the couple are renowned for their charitable giving. Established in 2000, the foundation has an endowment of well over $40 billion and has done admirable work throughout the world to enhance the quality of life of those who are in need. While at the visitor center, I read what I would consider to be the foundation's mission statement and broke down their game plan into three bullets:

- "Give our time, talents, and money to the causes we are passionate about."
- "Impact the next generation and beyond."
- "Focus on the greatest need."

They have a purpose, a calling, and a passion about what they do, and they have assimilated it into a strategy to increase the likelihood that it is executed successfully. For me, their game plan is preaching to the choir. If there is any disagreement, it is that we might differ in our interpretation of what is the world's "greatest need." Christian coaches have an alternate focus, as well as a different perspective on how and who might best facilitate the fulfillment of that need.

When I recruited, I began by asking each young man one simple question: what are the two or three most important things you are looking for in a university? That question enabled me to do a few things.

First, if we could not provide the things this person sought, I would disqualify myself and the university I represented. I would then offer to be an unbiased, third-party observer and help that person and their family find an institution that would meet their needs.

Second, if we did have what this individual desired, I would present that information to him. In either scenario, I would work with that person to help him remain focused on his goals so, regardless of the institution they chose, it would have the things he had declared were most important.

Christian coaches must always remember that life is a game—and we are constantly in play. In a dynamic world, Christian coaches must stay fixated on the one objective that separates us from the crowd: we must help the VPs that we transport to get from where they are to where they would like to be.

If the COVID-19 pandemic has taught us anything, it is that we must not only be focused, we must stay focused.

Game plans help initiate a path for the Christian coach; a process that brings the progress and a progression that leads a procession.

Never before have our plans become outdated so quickly. The coaching point from the quarantine is that coaches are only as good as their last game and we never know when the next game will be scheduled. Life is a variable, but our focus must remain fixed!

Game plans are blueprints for victory; this is the overriding takeaway for this chapter. Game plans help initiate a path for the Christian coach; a process that brings the progress and a progression that leads a procession.

7

MOVE UPWARD, OUTWARD, ONWARD

"You don't have to see the whole staircase, just take the first step."

Martin Luther King, Jr.

Unintentionally or strategically, one way or another, we take people with us. Christian coaching is a metaphor for discipleship. Our desire should be to create positive momentum through our actions; a thrust, if you will, to catapult us and others. It was a coaching concept that I learned in my early years.

As a child, I would frequently tag along to track meets to watch my father's teams compete. By far, my favorite event was the pole vault. For years, I dreamed of the day when I too would be able to jump like the athletes I so admired. When I finally reached the appropriate age in which to participate, there was no coach on our school's staff that had the knowledge I needed to show me how to vault. Initially, I researched the subject at the library and, for a brief while, my study proved to be fruitful. I was able to compete successfully, but as I aged, the competition grew fiercer.

In order to reach new heights, I needed improved technique, better than I was able to achieve on my own, but

I never received the coaching I sought. At times, I would launch myself well above the crossbar, easily clearing the height where it was set. However, on other attempts I would not even reach the apex of my arc, but instead land on the runway from which I made my approach (thankfully, on my feet). I needed a coach, someone to serve as a catalyst to help me reach new heights and move forward on my quest. To this day, I still wonder just how high I could have risen had I just received a little coaching.

For a Christian coach, as well as a pole vaulter, momentum is generated in two directions: upward and outward. Our inward transformation elicits an upward trajectory in our spiritual lives, while simultaneously producing an outward drive that serves as the impetus for the transportation of others on a similar spiritual launch. As we move in both directions, there is one thing of which we can be certain: we are not self-propelled. The thrust for our takeoff, and the power to continue our orbit, are not of our doing. Faith propels us skyward while trust pushes us forward; and trust is the basis for the confidence we need to possess to accomplish our spiritual goals. Trust trumps understanding.

When we board a flight, few of us understand how pilots operate the aircraft that carries us, but we trust them to transport us safely to our destination. In a similar manner, we might not understand why, how, or when, but we trust the Lord on each leg of our flight as well. For the apostles, trust certainly trumped understanding when they set out to feed five thousand with only two fish and five loaves of bread. To quote Warren Wiersbe, "Faith is a journey, and each happy destination is the beginning of a new journey." One phase after another, the Lord keeps us on track. It somewhat resembles an assembly line.

Manufacturing Coaches

To paraphrase a friend of mine, coaches implement the process that produces the progress, and our Heavenly Father does the same. The better the process, the greater the production, and the further the progress. In order to achieve this purpose, the Lord institutes a training regimen to orchestrate change in both directions for the coach—up and out.

Upward ("Stages")

To complete our training, He designs a discipleship pathway that takes us from point A to Z. The progression is the same for all, but the process is unique for each person. Typically, progressions take a tiered approach: sequentially ordered in increasing measures of complexity, intensity, and knowledge, but also benefit. For example, the training of a pilot begins in the classroom with an elementary introduction of the dashboard and advances to more complex instrumentation. He begins application with a simulator and then logs flight hours under the watchful eye of an accompanying instructor. Finally, he solos.

VPs need coaches to implement the transformational process in their own lives, so that they can provide the leadership that will produce the same spiritual growth in their lives. Regardless of the road we travel, our path will be marked by more than one fork. Some are more important than others, but each takes us somewhere, either toward an optimal conclusion or a bitter dead end.

We might turn to navigational devices for direction, but both the map and a GPS are worthless without a point of origin and a point of destination. Although we may begin our walk with Christ from a number of different entry points, all roads centered on Him lead to the same destination. If there is progress to be made, then a coach must ascertain where the VP is, point them to the goal, and assist them on their way.

If we use a manufacturing analogy, then the production of a Christian coach begins with input, followed by a system of operations, which leads to output. For a Christ follower, as was previously introduced, the process looks like this: we begin with a Saving Faith, which produces a Developing Faith, which begets a Living Faith, which results in Reaping Faith. Also known as justification, sanctification, and glorification, these are the stages the conveyor belt passes on the assembly line for all disciples.

Not only is this portion of the discipleship pathway a process, it is also the main cog of a cyclical progression. It is a generally accepted universal rule of behavior that rewarded actions will be repeated and, since we know that the Heavenly Father is faithful (2 Timothy 2:13), we can accurately predict that He will bless us accordingly. The elevation of our faith inspires the wheels of the progress to continue to churn. What we continue to reap, we will continue to sow. As our faith develops, there are more opportunities for its application and more rewards for us to reap. It is a process that perpetually progresses upward—one stage at a time.

Outward ("Steps")

Christian coaches are modern-day disciples. The training process that constructs a coach also constructs a leader. It is a leadership progression that promotes coach-making production. Transformation leads to transference! Regardless of the product that is produced—a disciple, doohickey, or thingamajig—output is enhanced through two coaching constructs: simplification and repetition. Your eyes did not deceive you. You read correctly: we want less and more at the same time. Simplification reduces the likelihood of error by reducing the number of steps.

Coaches know that fewer components require fewer actions, which means breakdowns are less likely to occur. For example, there are many movable parts involved in the act of throwing a football. In the many years that I trained quarterbacks, I became more proficient in training them in this all-important aspect of their position. By breaking down their throwing mechanics, I was able to increase their ability to perform.

Conversely, repetition produces economies of scale. The more frequently we engage, the more we take advantage of the coaching opportunities we are afforded, and the better we become at fabricating coaches. Whatever the task, subtraction (simplification) and addition (repetition) lead to productivity. For a quarterback to efficiently deliver a football to his intended target, he needs to concentrate on four areas: feet, trunk rotation, arm speed, and the release point of the football. For the successful migration of a coach and VP, their portion of the pathway can be broken down into four sections: Engage, Escort, Equip, and Empower.

The production of a disciple is accomplished through the leadership of a coach. It is a leadership progression that produces a discipleship procession and coaching succession! And, it is the part of the manufacturing process that continually looks outward.

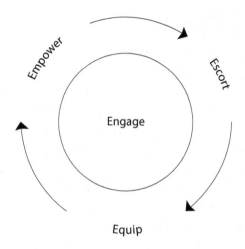

In order for the coach's leadership to be effective, both wheels of the coach-making conveyor need to spin. One without the other brings the entire production line to a screeching halt. As Christian coaches manufacture disciples, not unlike an assembly line, our goal is not just to operate without interruption, but to accelerate the wheels of production, so that output might be increased.

The Disciple-Making Process and Progression

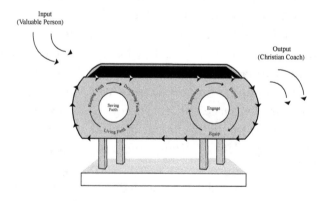

(Model is a modified version of a Man-in-the-Mirror graphic.)

Onward ("Stairs")

Finally, the Christian coach is both the driver and a vehicle on the discipleship highway. He is both a means of delivery and the valuable commodity that is delivered. To generate progress for the coach and the VP along the discipleship pathway, the Lord works within us and through us, internally and externally, to accomplish His will. Internally it is about transformation, while externally it is about transportation. The Lord's objective is to always take us to a new place—to a higher level and a more advanced state. There's a vertical and a horizontal movement in the life of a coach, both latitude and longitude components. God builds us up in order to ship us out. Transformation and transportation plot the trajectory of our lives.

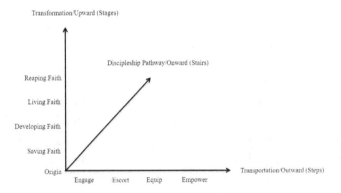

A Christian coach is a factor of both elevation and extension! The pathway of the coach must incorporate both depth and width! You can't advance by having one without the other. Transformation alone lacks width. If we don't extend ourselves, we do not advance our calling. Transportation by itself lacks depth. If we don't elevate spiritually, we do not fulfill our purpose. We handicap ourselves and others when we do not embrace transformation and transportation.

Together, they mark the elevation and extension coordinates for the slope of our ascension. From our point of spiritual origin, to our heavenly destination, Christian coaches traverse upward, outward, and onward along the discipleship pathway. It seems there really is a "stairway to heaven" after all.

Building and Walking Take Time

There are two metaphors that accurately describe and emphasize the transformation and transportation elements in the life of a coach: building and walking.

"You also, like living stones, are being built into a spiritual house to be a holy priesthood…" (1 Peter 2:5).

"Whoever claims to abide in Him must walk as Jesus walked" (1 John 2:6 Berean Study Bible)

Scripture attests that there is both an elevation that we are to assume and a route in which we are to proceed. There are steps (Outward) that need to be taken and stages (Upward) that need to be completed to draw closer to our goal.

By definition, ascension gradually moves us to a more advanced state, but it is not only about the destination, it is about the journey as well. We tell ourselves that "If I only get to here, then I will be happy," so we do everything in our power to get there as fast as we can. However, that is not how it works. It takes time to reach a worthwhile destination. It is a walk, not a race; smaller steps, and preliminary stages, are designed to build our stride and accelerate our pace. We'd like to be like characters in *Star Trek* and instantaneously be "beamed" to our journey's end. But if we were teleported to the end, we would miss the adventure along the way. As Carl Lewis once said, "It's all about the journey, not the outcome." If we just beamed aboard, we would miss all the opportunities to witness God's grace as we travel.

Life is a staircase (Onward); we begin at the bottom and, through the guidance of our Savior, there is a pinnacle toward which we will rise and a podium on which we will eventually stand. If we are patient, what begins as a walk is built into a sprint. And our Master Coach will remove any hitch in our gait.

Acceleration: You Must Learn How to Walk Before You Can Run

Wilma did not set out to become a world-class athlete; for her that just was not an option. When she began to train it was not in the hopes of attaining an Olympic medal; it was merely in hopes of being able to walk once more. Growing up in poverty in rural Tennessee, during a period of racial segregation, Wilma was barely afforded more than the basic amenities of life. As the twentieth of her father's twenty-two children, she did not have much more than food on the table, a roof over her head, and dresses made from flour sacks, but scarcity can build tenacity (as well as a great perspective). "Believe me," she once said, "the reward is not so great without the struggle," and during her lifetime Wilma knew both reward and struggle on a first-name basis.[1]

The challenges that Wilma overcame would have precluded most people from ever entertaining thoughts of athletic achievement, let alone from envisioning world records, but not Wilma. For Wilma they were not delusions of grandeur, but realities too grand for dissolution. In addition to poverty and prejudice that were pervasive in the culture in which she was raised, her childhood was also one beset by illness—measles, mumps, scarlet fever, chicken pox, and even double pneumonia. As the saying goes, "If she did not have bad luck, she would have no luck at all."

Wilma overcame one sickness after another, but these illnesses were mere setbacks compared to the polio infection she contracted at four years of age. In the 1940s and 1950s, the number of polio cases that were reported grew to epidemic proportions.[2] Worldwide, more than a half million people either died or were left paralyzed each year as a result of this debilitating disease, and Wilma had just been added to this long list of names.

The crippling infection left Wilma's left leg and foot weak and deformed, and her family's financial constraints limited her chances of recovery even more. Since her mother had no money to pay for the care of a local doctor, they traveled fifty miles every other week to a clinic they could afford. When they finally did see a physician, the prognosis was not good, but Wilma chose to listen to a different prognosticator. Wilma said, "My doctor told me I would never walk again. My mother told me I would. I believed my mother."

Her mother formed a makeshift metal brace for her to wear for support and enlisted Wilma's brothers and sisters as her physical therapists. Together, her mom and her siblings provided Wilma with all the coaching she would need to prevail. From their home, her family members directed Wilma through a series of exercises until finally, after two years of treatments, they saw progress. Wilma took her first step. It was not until she was twelve years old that she would once again walk normally, but Wilma wanted to do more than just walk—she wanted to run.

It would be an understatement to say that she lacked athletic prowess at the outset. Take basketball, for instance. Basketball was Wilma's first love, but in her first three years on the basketball team she did not play in one single game. She might have turned to track and field, but her all-black high school had no track team for which she could run. But it would take more than the absence of a track team to stop her from running. Wilma ran; my, how she ran. Wilma Rudolph ran all the way to the 1960 Olympic Games in Rome, Italy, and she did so in spectacular fashion by becoming the first American woman, and the first African American woman, to win three gold medals in a single Olympiad.

The sprinting sensation had reached the pinnacle for track and field and, when she retired two years later, she did so as the world record holder in the 100- and 200-meter dash and as the anchor leg for the fastest 4x100-meter relay time ever recorded. The young girl who once could not walk had become the fastest woman in the world, but few knew of the painstaking process it took to get there.

Like Wilma, we must be able to learn to walk before we can run. Life experience is attained through a series of steps and stages that we take with confidence in the Lord Almighty. We need both: together, they form a stairway. Shortcuts may promise a quicker route by reducing our steps, but they can sabotage the very thing we seek. Instant millionaires frequently go broke. Those thrown into the deep end must be prepared to swim or they will sink.

Stages are equally important. They bolster our purpose and calling. God says He has many things in store for us in the future, but we do not want to lose sight of the here and now. Take Moses, for example. When Moses peered into the future, he only did so as one who "was looking ahead to his reward" rather than "enjoying the fleeting pleasures of sin" (Hebrews 11:26, 25). He did not dwell upon what was to be; it only motivated him to live well in the present. In time, we will be able to look back upon the pathway that has led to our advance and exclaim, "As for God, His way is perfect" (2 Samuel 22:31). The Lord will get you where you need to be when you need to be there. On the discipleship pathway, don't bypass the process in favor of an escalator, elevator, or any other more expedient route. Take the stairs!

8

MOVE UPWARD

"You're no longer wandering exiles. This kingdom of faith is now your home country. You're no longer strangers or outsiders. You belong here, with as much right to the name Christian as anyone. God is building a home. He's using us all—irrespective of how we got here—in what he is building. He used the apostles and prophets for the foundation. Now he's using you, fitting you in brick by brick, stone by stone, with Christ Jesus as the cornerstone that holds all the parts together. We see it taking shape day after day—a holy temple built by God, all of us built into it, a temple in which God is quite at home."

Ephesians 2:19-22 MSG

**Purpose: A Transformation Model
"The Construction of a Coach"**

Some Assembly Required

Let's switch up our sports metaphor of developing a coach to a trade motif. The coach begins like an apprentice. At this point, the beginning tradesmen yield themselves to a series of on-the-job exercises designed to reproduce the skills that are demonstrated by the masters in their field. Carefully, a training process is crafted so that the pupils might ascend safely toward their educational goal.

If they faithfully follow the curriculum set out for them, they will advance to the next phase in the program. If not, they must repeat the lesson until they demonstrate the proficiency necessary for promotion. When the training is completed, the trainee may then become a trainer of future apprentices.

Whereas the training course for an apprentice is founded on a trade, the training regimen for a coach and the VP they transport is founded on faith. Faith is the opposite of empirical evidence. Only in absence can it be verified; something must be lacking for it to be applied. Faith is the cement that fills in the cracks of that which is unknown or cannot be explained. It unites us to God's trusted representatives of the past (see Hebrews 11), binds us to our fellow Christ followers, and connects us to the VP.

While Paul affirms that there is "one faith" that unites the body of Christ (Ephesians 4:5), Peter confirms that all Christ followers are enrolled in an apprenticeship program: "So don't lose a minute in building on what you've been given. Make every effort to add to your faith" (2 Peter 1:5 MSG/NIV).

The addition of faith comes under the tutelage of the Master Builder, who provides personalized instruction. His lesson plans include periodic exams that enable the coach to demonstrate that his faith sticks. Although each test is unique, the template used by the Master Builder is the same.

First, He creates a void. Then He mixes the elements within the coach to produce an adhesive compound capable of patching the gap. Only by bridging the gap can the apprentice coach pass the exam and take the next step of faith. As James writes, "Faith by itself, if it is not accompanied by action, is dead" (2:17). For the apprentice coach to progress to greater levels of service, he must be able to "apply" faith at each interval of testing.

Romans says that our actions—or inactions—always lead us somewhere; like a staircase, we either ascend or descend: "For whatsoever is not of faith is sin" (14:23 KJV). It's black and white; there is no gray area. We either grow by faith or we grow in our sin. Only when we exercise our faith can we climb the stairs of advancement.

To construct a Christian coach, the Master Builder utilizes a four-part training process to ensure that we progress upward.

1. Saving Faith: Faith in Jesus Christ and God's Word
2. Developing Faith: Faith in God that inspires our spiritual growth
3. Living Faith: Faith that the Holy Spirit will enable us to fulfill our calling
4. Reaping Faith: Faith that God will reward our efforts

Each level that is constructed is built upon the last and results not just in an average coach, but "God's masterpiece" (Ephesians 2:10 NLT)

If we Christian coaches faithfully submit ourselves to His training process, like the apprentice, we will be shaped and molded into the image of the Master and we too will train future coaching apprentices in the faith. As A.W. Tozer put it, "With the goodness of God to desire our highest welfare, the wisdom of God to plan it, and the power of God to achieve it, what do we lack?"

Saving Faith

Saving faith is the equivalent of breaking ground. It's more than ceremonial; it is the spiritual unearthing of a new Christian coach. As coaches interact with the VP, saving faith becomes the VP's entry point for transforming into coaches themselves. But, the coach's duties do not conclude when the one we coach becomes a Christ follower. Christian coaches will continue to transport the new believers as they progress on their discipleship pathway. Together, they both grow in their faith.

When we surrender our lives to Jesus Christ, excavation of a new Christian coach begins. The building site is cleared so that construction might begin. Jesus removes the debris from our past and begins to build the foundation of a new life. There need not be another groundbreaking; construction is underway.

Developing Faith

While saving faith is the critical first element in the construction of a Christian coach, we need more than a good foundation to build a life of significance.

A former neighbor of mine provides a great illustration to make my point. In this older neighborhood each home had a garage located behind it and an alley that provided communal access to each garage. One day, as I left for work, I noticed the tenants behind us were dismantling their garage. Neatly, the gentleman disassembled every plank and stacked them to the side. The planks were well worn, the paint chipped. Even intact the garage had appeared as if one good gust of wind might topple the structure once and for all.

When he was done tearing apart the garage, he proceeded to pour the concrete base on the area where the building formerly stood.

However, after his solid cement foundation had dried, what I saw next took me by surprise. Plank by plank, this man took the dilapidated wood that had been set aside and reconstructed the garage to its original state. Although the new floor gave the gentleman a more secure foundation, what he built on it was certainly suspect. This provided me a coaching principle that I have remembered ever since: you can't just rest on your foundation, you must wisely build upon it. Whatever you build, if you want it to last, you must intentionally develop it.

How do you eat an elephant? We all know that the answer is one bite at a time. In like fashion, our faith is developed one step at a time and one day at a time. Jesus "said to them all: 'If anyone would come after me, he must deny himself and take up his cross daily and follow me. For whoever wants to save his life will lose it, but whoever loses his life for me will save it'" (Luke 9:23-24 NIV '84). Faith must be renewed daily. Because you exercised it yesterday does not mean you have arrived. It's a series of choices that lead to a final destination, and it begins and ends on our knees.

Faith is a matter of man's submission and God's intervention. As Christian coaches, when we submit ourselves to the Heavenly Father, He works through the Holy Spirit who indwells us to increase our faith. While our spiritual maturity might experience a growth spurt due to dramatic circumstances that are the allegorical cross Christ said that we might bear, typically they occur gradually as we exercise daily spiritual disciplines. Bible study, prayer, and additional research we conduct, such as examination of apologetics and historical insights, further build upon our base. Similar to the physiological changes that occur as we develop from infancy to physical maturity, our faith develops subtly over time.

If we see an individual almost every day, changes are more difficult to discern. However, if a span of time exists between encounters, the changes in individuals become more prominent. How many of us have marveled at the growth of our nieces and nephews when we are reunited with them after a period in which we had been separated?

If it is difficult to notice the physical growth in our children whom we see regularly, how much more challenging must it be to discern our own spiritual maturation? It would be nice if we could set up a GoPro camera to record a time-lapse video to verify the positive development that is so difficult to ascertain. When played back, it would unveil the prominence of the transformation and no doubt inspire the disciple at the same time.

Furthermore, there are two external forces that want to stand in the way of our spiritual advancement: the world and the enemy. But we have a proclivity to undermine our development as well. As Christian coaches, we often do not detect our own growth because we are our harshest critic. We withhold self praise, either because we believe that personal humility mandates it or we have a negative perception of ourselves. While we may not be where we would like to be spiritually, we also are not where we once were. God is not done with our assembly! Coaches are a work that is still ongoing, and others will begin to take notice of the stark contrast as they witness our fabrication.

As our faith develops, our testimony begins to take shape. The Lord states that we are built for illumination: "I'm setting you up as a light for the nations so that my salvation becomes global!" (Isaiah 49:6 MSG). All the events that occur in our lives are meant to elevate our faith, so that Christ might become visible to more people.

Living Faith

We are never more visible than when we experience obstacles in our lives, so the Master Coach will frequently subject us to intense pressure so that He might be illuminated more. Before we are able to coach others, the Lord will put us through a battery of tests to strengthen our reliance on Him, and the resolve we will need to deliver victory to our VPs. Coaches drill their athletes and use scrimmages to prepare them to succeed. Strategically, I would often "stack the deck" against an athlete in practice, so that he would be immune from the pressure of the game. I called it "Inoculation Training."

For example, I would often place our field goal kicker in a situation at practice that would simulate a game-winning kick. "If you make the kick," I would tell him, "the team will not have to run sprints after practice. However, if you miss the kick, the team will run twice as many sprints."

To ensure that the defense would try their best to disrupt the field goal attempt, I would tell them that they would not have to run any sprints if they blocked the kick. Sometimes, the result was a very tired team after the field goal attempt, and sometimes our kicker was lifted high onto his teammates' shoulders in celebration.

There is one final point I would like to make from this illustration. In my ten years as the head football coach at Charleston Southern University, whenever the game was on the line, whether it be on the last play of regulation or in overtime, our field goal kickers never missed! Our Master Coach knows even better how to train us for a successful coaching career.

Faith does not stand still; it's about activity, not acknowledgment. Words are meaningless—what the framers of our Bill of Rights would call a "parchment guarantee"— unless they are accompanied by action.

When they created the Bill of Rights, our American forefathers knew that they must defend its contents for it to be effective. There are dictatorships that have produced more impressive documents, with more eloquent words regarding individual rights, but those governments never followed through on what they promised. They were merely guarantees on parchment paper, and since they were never enforced, they were not worth the ink and the paper on which they were printed.

Parchment guarantees are the equivalent of a tree that fails to bear fruit: both are worthless and deserve a similar fate. Jesus uses the analogy of a fruitless tree to describe an unfaithful disciple and the consequence that results from their inactivity: "The ax is already at the root of the trees, and every tree that does not produce good fruit will be cut down and thrown into the fire" (Matthew 3:10). Faithful disciples produce fruit. They do more than talk a good game; unlike a parchment guarantee, they let their "'yes' be 'yes,' and [their] 'no' be 'no'" (Matthew 5:37 HCSB). Coaches follow through; they are living and breathing disciples of Jesus Christ, and their activity is generated through a respiratory system that works.

Anatomically, activity in the human body is produced through a combination of voluntary and involuntary muscles. As part of the autonomic nervous system, we have no conscious control over the physiological mechanisms that occur in our bodies; they are completely involuntary. Conversely, voluntary muscles can be consciously controlled and manipulated at our will. Although physiologically our breathing can fluctuate, it involuntarily continues as long as we do. When we stop breathing, we stop living. Literally and figuratively, there are two ways that we can suffocate: by not being able to breathe in and by not being able to breathe out.

As Christ followers, figuratively speaking, our respiratory system is entirely voluntary. We control our breathing. Our Creator assembled us to both inhale and exhale. We inhale when do the things that develop us spiritually, and we exhale when we serve the Lord wholeheartedly. Christian coaches must do both in order to live faithfully and reap a reward.

Reaping Faith

A Christ follower receives blessing, reward, and favor as they walk by faith. Each is distinctive, and each provides a promise for today and the hope for tomorrow. Awards are distributed to Christ followers in three ways:

- Immediately
- Comprehensively
- Contingently

Ephesians promises that we receive "every spiritual blessing" (1:3) immediately and comprehensively through Jesus Christ when we profess Him to be our Savior and Redeemer. These are not just something we look forward to receiving in heaven; they are ours to be enjoyed while on earth. Christ assures us of an abundant life (John 10:10) in this lifetime, and Peter confirms this when he says, "His divine power has given us everything we need" (2 Peter 1:3). Rewards, blessing, and favor are ours on earth and in heaven; we reap here and now, and there and then.

Rewards, blessing, and favor are ours on earth and in heaven; we reap here and now, and there and then.

God's Word also promises that blessings will be distributed in eternity contingent upon what we do during our lifetime on earth. Paul reminds us that our actions today will have consequences forever when he writes that "we must all stand before Christ to be judged. We will each receive whatever we deserve for the good or evil we have done in this earthly body" (2 Corinthians 5:10 NLT). As we obediently serve Jesus Christ, we can count on receiving "an inheritance from the Lord" (Colossians 3:24) that will be eternally ours.

While the pursuit of heavenly reward should be a lifelong quest on the part of each and every disciple, I would be remiss if I did not point out that we will be eternally joyful, regardless the size of the bounty we amass. Dr. Wayne Grudem said it best:

> Although there will be degrees of reward in heaven, the joy of each person will be full and complete for eternity. If we ask how this can be when there are different degrees of reward, it simply shows that our perception of happiness is based on the assumption that happiness depends on what we possess or the status or power that we have. In actuality, however, our true happiness consists in delighting in God and rejoicing in the status and recognition that He has given us. The foolishness of thinking that only those who have been highly rewarded and given great status will be fully happy in heaven is seen when we realize that no matter how great a reward we are given, there will always be those with greater rewards, or who have higher status and authority, including the apostles, the heavenly creatures, and Jesus Christ and God Himself. Therefore, if highest status were essential for people to be fully happy, no one but God would be fully happy in heaven, which is certainly an incorrect idea. Moreover, those with greater reward and honor in heaven, those nearest the throne of God, delight not in their status but only in the privilege of falling down before God's throne to worship Him.[1]

Finally, it is the Lord's favor that enables a Christian coach's work to be accomplished. It is received by grace and affirms that the work we do was divinely assigned. God's favor is not confirmed by our prosperity or repudiated because of our difficulties. Many faithful disciples experienced hardship yet were favored by the Lord. Daniel was looked upon with favor while in captivity (Daniel 1:9). The Lord showed favor on Joseph by altering the perspective of the jailers while he was imprisoned (Genesis 39:21). And it was favor that Mary received when God selected her to be the unwed mother of the Messiah (Luke 1:30).

Every noble work recorded in Scripture was originated in favor, executed in faith, and resulted in glory to God. As Christian coaches, our work will be accomplished in similar fashion and preserved in the heavenly annals: "You saw me before I was born. Every day of my life was recorded in your book. Every moment was laid out before a single day had passed" (Psalm 139:16 NLT).

Now or later, full or measured, Christ followers will not reap blessings, rewards, and favor without saving, developing, and living faith. The writer of Hebrews confirms this: "Without faith it is impossible to please God, because anyone who comes to him must believe that he exists and that he rewards those who earnestly seek him" (Hebrews 11:6 NIV '84).

As we journey, we must remember to stay on the path! The reward is not just for that which we have accomplished, it is in the pursuit as well. The blessings we accumulate from a life of faith are not just for us as individuals, but are for the whole of God's people. Blessings are for coach who fears God and walks in His ways, and for the VPs he transports on his pilgrimage.

> All you who fear God, how blessed you are! how happily you walk on his smooth straight road! You worked hard and deserve all you've got coming. Enjoy the blessing! Revel in the goodness!
>
> Your wife will bear children as a vine bears grapes, your household lush as a vineyard, The children around your table as fresh and promising as young

olive shoots. Stand in awe of God's Yes. Oh, how he blesses the one who fears God!

Enjoy the good life in Jerusalem every day of your life. And enjoy your grandchildren. Peace to Israel! (Psalm 128 MSG)

In a nutshell, blessings are for the whole, for future generations, and for us to enjoy now and for eternity! Blessing, reward, and favor inspire us to get up, get moving, and get to work. "Let the favor of the Lord our God be upon us, and establish the work of our hands upon us; yes, establish the work of our hands!" (Psalm 90:17 ESV).

Paul promises us, "And I am certain that God, who began the good work within you, will continue his work until it is finally finished on the day when Christ Jesus returns" (Philippians 1:6 NLT). We know the endgame; we need a well-rounded training regimen that will bring it about.

9

BULK UP

"He will be the sure foundation for your times, a rich store of salvation and wisdom and knowledge; the fear of the Lord is the key to this treasure."

Isaiah 33:6

Coaches must train themselves to be godly in order to train others similarly. They spiritually bulk up so they can "carry their own load" and "carry each other's burdens" as well (Galatians 6:5, 2). "For physical training is of some value, but godliness has value for all things, holding promise for both the present life and the life to come" (1 Timothy 4:8). Physical training will be helpful for a season, but sooner or later, age catches up with us all. On the other hand, spiritual training transcends time, such as in the sessions and lessons shared by Paul to Timothy. The apostle urges his young protégé to train "in season and out of season" (2 Timothy 4:2), but what he is really saying is that there is no off-season. As Christian coaches, our service is 24/7/365. Let the transformation begin!

Fundamentals: Putting First Things First

Basketball legend Michael Jordan taught, "Get the fundamentals down and the level of everything you do will rise."

Not too long ago, my former church scheduled a softball game as part of its men's ministry. A young adult, wishing to participate in the game but needing lessons in the basics, sought out coaching from one of the senior members of our church family. Growing up, this twenty-year-old did not have a father active in his life, so he missed out on the wonderful bonding experience that most boys have had by playing catch with their fathers. Knowing that the young man had never learned how to throw, the older gentleman gladly accommodated his request and assumed the surrogate role.

As you might have guessed, initially it did not go very well. With a glove on his left hand and the ball in his right, the novice hurled the ball everywhere but directly to the glove of his playing partner. The mentor would have needed to be a major league ballplayer to have had a chance at fielding some of the errant throws. The instructor actually spent more time, and exerted more energy, retrieving the ball than he did playing catch, but eventually his pupil did manage to get the ball closer to his mitt. All in all, it was a productive session so the two men discussed plans for additional training. As they left the ball field together that day, the shy young man had just one question for his mentor: "Does it make any difference that I am left-handed?"

Like the true story just shared, Christian coaches won't get very far if we don't settle important matters at the outset. If we don't stand for something, we will fall for anything, but I would add that if we don't stand for the right thing, all that we hold dear could collapse. There are matters fundamental to our existence, critical paths in everything we do.

Professionally, I don't care what your vocation may be; there are basics that are fundamental to your success. For example, if you are an accountant, then you know that debits must equal credits and that a balance sheet must always balance. If you're Christian coach, you also know that there have got to be some basics we establish that, when practiced, will strengthen our development. William James once said, "The art of being wise is the art of knowing what to overlook." A wise coach will not overlook the fundamentals.

Before any coach begins to lead his or her team, they must not just be vaguely familiar with the material they are presenting. They must continue to study so that they might become "thoroughly equipped" on the subject matter (2 Timothy 3:17). Coaches study a playbook in order to understand the terminology, transfer their knowledge to their pupils, and prepare answers for the inevitable questions that will be asked. The coach's playbook includes spiritual disciplines of prayer and Bible study. They are the basics upon which a coach is trained.

Prayer

Ephesians 6:18 teaches us to "Pray in the Spirit at all times and on every occasion. Stay alert and be persistent in your prayers for all believers everywhere" (NLT).

In the early morning fog cast over the Charles River, I used to watch the men and women of the Harvard crew team practice. With precise synchronization, their oars would strike the water time and time again, always acting in unison. As I watched, the skulls would slice through the water with the ease of a knife through butter. But, what fascinated me the most was the fact that the oarsmen never saw the direction they were heading. Their backs remained to their destination while all leadership was coalesced squarely on the shoulders of one lone person—the coxswain.

As the only individual facing forward, the coxswain assumes all responsibility for the navigation of the vessel. Literally, his team follows him blindly as he sits on his perch. Like the conductor of a symphony, he sets the tempo while his oarsmen act as an orchestra to maintain the beat. Together, they create a type of composition on the water.

The coxswain also determines their direction. The eyes of the oarsmen look up to him and their ears fixate on his voice. Vocally, he builds them up and encourages them to press on. Visually, he steers them to the finish line. Each time the oarsmen enter the watercraft, they trust the coxswain will lead them toward a new and exciting opportunity. In fact, the word "opportunity" is Latin in origin and means "toward the port." As Christ followers, each day we are promised a new racing adventure that is guaranteed to transport us "toward the port."

As we row through the waters of this life, our faith is to be placed upward, and that trust propels us forward. We stroke "by faith, not by sight" (2 Corinthians 5:7), reliant on the One at our helm. No matter how rough the water might become, the Lord will navigate us safely to our heavenly dock. As Christian coaches, our communication with our Navigator must not be interrupted; we must focus to hear His commands and coordinate with our teammates to row in unison toward our common goal. We can count on our Master Coxswain to steer the coach and the VP toward a wave of opportunities—All aboard!

An Elevated Perspective

Athletic coaches have long stated that "the eye in the sky does not lie." It's a phrase that usually references the video that is being shot to record every movement of the athlete's performance. The camera negates any excuse that might be given, because the truth is available for all to see. Early on, athletes and their coaches learn that, to increase the likelihood of a desired result, we should look above for helpful clues. Better yet, if we can stay in constant communication with one who has an elevated perspective, that person can help us see what we cannot see from our vantage point, and they can guide us on the best possible route toward our goal.

For the Christian coach, prayer connects us with our infallible Eye in the Sky. From creation to completion, prayer is instrumental in executing our game plan! As Christ followers, you realize early on that, when God moves, you must follow, but you can only do so by remaining alert. It is a biblically based coaching principle. Only when you "devote yourselves to prayer, being watchful and thankful" (Colossians 4:2), will you be assured of not missing an all-important call.

In the 2010 Winter Olympics, German speed skater Patrick Beckert represented his country as an alternate in the 1000m competition. Unexpectedly, the two-time gold medalist in the event withdrew one hour before his preliminary heat, providing Beckert the opportunity he had thought was too foolish to entertain. However, since withdrawal was so unlikely, Beckert's coach failed to instruct his speed skater to report to the racing oval just in case such an event might occur. Frantically, the coach tried to contact him to let him know he had now been elevated to active status, but all to no avail. Beckert had turned off his cell phone. Ninety-nine times out of one hundred an alternate would not have the opportunity to replace an Olympic gold medalist, but faith means in spite of the odds.[1]

The story provides two coaching points. First, we must keep an open line of communication with our Heavenly Father, no matter what. If we do not answer the call, like Beckert, we might miss the opportunity of a lifetime. Second, when the coach fails, the VP fails. When we fail to answer our calling, the repercussions are felt by others. One way or another, our lives impact those in our vicinity.

In the days before cell phones, my wife and I went out for the evening and left our three-year-old daughter in the capable hands of my younger brother—or so I thought. During dinner, I excused myself and placed a phone call to check in and see how they were both doing. At the other end of the line I encountered an uncle who frantically wanted to know the answer to one question. Apparently, my daughter had been fussing for the entire two hours of our absence, because she had not received satisfaction to her one request. Repeatedly, she had said, "I want a wid!" The obvious question posed by my brother, her uncle, was "What's a wid?" I immediately was able to translate what was to him a foreign dialect. What his niece was trying to enunciate was that she wanted a lid for her sippy cup. The reason my brother couldn't understand her, the reason he couldn't respond to her request, was because she wasn't his child—she didn't belong to him. As Christ followers, we belong to our Heavenly Father and He always understands what we tell Him.

As believers, we speak the same language; we are heard and we are able to hear—and comprehend—more as we build on the foundation of Jesus Christ and keep an open line of communication. He may answer yes, no, or not yet. Regardless of the response, we can trust that what He is constructing in us will be in our best interest.

Bible Study

Not only am I challenged mechanically in the trade crafts, I am technically challenged as well. Shortly before I retired from coaching, I acquired iPads for each of my assistant coaches and myself to use in recruiting. Knowing my limitations, our business manager purchased a text titled *iPads for Dummies*. I wasn't offended; I was thankful that she purchased the book to help me learn how to use what was at the time, a new device. However, as I began to read the book, it became obvious that I knew even less than she could have predicted. I needed a book to help me understand how to use this book!

What do you do when you do not understand a book that was written for dummies? Even worse, how do you return a book with that title and explain to the person in customer service that it was over your head? I envisioned that ensuing interaction in my mind and suddenly realized I was not alone. The late comedian Mitch Hedberg once had a similar experience, and he also dreaded the exchange he imagined he would have with the customer service representative. Like Mitch, I, too, was confident the representative would ask, "What are you, a dummy?" My only honest response to that question had to be, "I wish! I aspire to be a dummy. Right now I'm just an imbecile." Thanks to some wonderful assistants I have had over the years, I have received the support I needed, but there is one book that has all the answers I need; and I can read it all by myself.

The Whole Truth and Nothing but the Truth

In her comedic repertoire, Lily Tomlin frequently played a fictitious character named Edith Ann. Holding a lollipop as a prop, she would sit in an oversized rocker to give the appearance that she was a five-year-old girl. Seated from her lofty perch, Lily Tomlin would share stories about her family and spout pearls of wisdom from the perspective of a little girl. Interspersed in her comments were granules of truth laced with embellishment and wild imagination. As intended, the character's reasoning prompted laughter from the audience, especially when she concluded each skit of fabrication with the same four words: "And that's the truth!"

It was obvious to everyone, except maybe the character of Edith Ann, that she had misplaced the truth.

Misplaced or not, one thing both genders seek is truth. As He prayed for His disciples, Jesus revealed its location: "Sanctify them by the truth; your Word is truth" (John 17:17). These are marching orders for the Christian coach, so we must equip ourselves for the task. We don't need to search for it, because it is right under our noses. It doesn't need to be identified or invented; it just needs to be ingested.

Truth is a foundational element in the construction of the Christian coach, and French scholar Isaac Casaubon expresses that it is much more than that. "Truth is the foundation of all knowledge and the cement of all society." If it is that important—and I am convinced that it is—then when we find it, we should secure a grip and never let go. But let go is exactly what Harvard University did.

Founded in 1836, Harvard University is the oldest institution of higher learning in our country. Originally, the college was created to serve as a training ground for ministers so that the gospel might be dispersed throughout the new frontier. Named after its first benefactor, Pastor John Harvard, the initial school seal was emblazoned on a shield and contained the words *Veritas Christo et Ecclesiae* (Latin for "Truth for Christ and the Church"). Its crest, on which the seal rested, displayed the outline of three books. Two of the books faced up (one represented Jesus Christ, the source of all truth; the other extolled the virtues of education). The third book was laid facedown, expressing that there were limits to man's knowledge. One of the finest and most recognizable universities in the world began with a clear mission, but over time both the school shield and its understanding of truth would begin to erode.

Today, the university's emblem looks quite different. The third book has now been turned faceup and Harvard's seal contains only one word: *Veritas*. The symbolism of the revision cannot be misinterpreted—it professes that human reasoning is now all that we need; there is no need for the divine because we can count exclusively on our intellect. In Harvard's quest for truth, they eliminated the one source from which it could be obtained, and, in doing so, they are now further away from that which they aspire than when they first began.[2]

Truth on the Trading Block

In professional sports, it is not uncommon for organizations to trade athletes. Through such an exchange, team management hopes to strengthen their squad. But only history will record whether the transaction was foolish or wise. When it comes to information, Christian coaches must qualify the source. Even "the foolishness of God is wiser than human wisdom, and the weakness of God is stronger than human strength" (I Corinthians 1:25). Team Harvard is not the only institution of advanced learning to stumble on their journey toward truth. Universities, and individuals alike, can negate that which they desire to attain if they remove God from the equation. Truth has been transcribed, but the reason for their loss is they have gone to the wrong playbook—or should I say textbook?

While driving through San Francisco a few summers ago, I observed banners advertising the University of Pennsylvania's prestigious Wharton School of Business that read, "Learn from the people who wrote the textbooks." I could not have agreed more! Repeatedly, leadership expert, Charlie Jones emphasized the significance of that which was on our reading list when he said, "You will be the same person you are today in five years but for two things: the people you meet and the books you read."

Many are proponents of education and I am certainly one of them. But, while education undeniably provides benefits that extend into every aspect of our lives, it is incomplete and cannot be exclusively relied upon.

For instance, during my senior year in high school, I thought it might be wise to register for an elective course that would prepare me for all the papers I anticipated I would be required to submit in college, so I signed up for a class titled *Research and Expository Writing*. The semester-long course culminated with a term paper that would account for a majority of my class grade. I chose to write an exposé on the assassination of John F. Kennedy. Although I put a lot of time and effort into the project, sadly, I only received a C+ grade. In my first semester in college, my Political Science 101 course also required a term paper.

When I saw the parameters of what was stipulated on the syllabus, it dawned on me that I could submit the same paper that I had just turned in for my high school English course less than six months earlier. After all, I reasoned, since it was my work, I could not plagiarize myself. I only needed to change the cover page to finish this assignment. To me, it was an efficient decision that would afford me the opportunity to concentrate on courses that required more of my time.

When the professor returned our essays, I smiled when I saw the mark that I received—it was a B. I knew I should have received a better grade in high school, but the story does not end there. Can you guess what happened when I pursued a Master's degree? Once again, changing only the cover page, the mark I received on my high school term paper became an A as part of my postgraduate work! Maybe this is why I chose to forego a doctorate degree—it just wouldn't have been worth the effort I would have had to expend to receive an A+!

Dr. Angela Duckworth, Professor of Psychology at the University of Pennsylvania, said, "As a scientist, I'm tempted to answer that we need more research on the topic."[3] The same logic could be applied to any number of topics. Regardless the subject matter, Paul predicted a similar conclusion nearly 2000 years ago when he said that some will always be, "learning but never able to come to a knowledge of the truth" (2 Timothy 3:7).

Education will never give us all the answers we desire and its accuracy has proven to be questionable. Those spewing wisdom similar to Edith Ann, expounding words intended to convince today's audience of their "truth," will only have future generations retract their messages and brand them as misguided.

Believe it or not, at one time a German pharmaceutical company marketed a drug that they contended would be a non-addictive answer for those who had a simple cough. It wasn't until the 20th century that the slightly embarrassed company discovered that the medicine they promoted actually metabolized into morphine in the human body. The drug was heroin and the company that promoted its use is still around today—Bayer.[4] In search of life's answers, education can only take us so far.

The coach that constructs their life on prayer and His infallible Word, sets a direct course with an upward trajectory. It's spiritually fundamental. And that's the truth!

10

KNOW THE OPPOSITION

"Look straight ahead, and fix your eyes on what lies before you. Mark out a straight path for your feet; stay on the safe path. Don't get sidetracked; keep your feet from following evil."

Proverbs 4:25-27 NLT

Before an athletic contest, coaches will often send a staff member to view a future opponent's game so that they can create a scouting report on that opponent. After all, we have to know what we're looking for to train ourselves to be on the lookout. Coaches need to study the techniques and strategies their opponents will attempt to utilize to tilt the game in their favor, and they need to train those they lead to anticipate these maneuvers as well.

Tells

Sports enthusiasts have always looked for an advantage. In baseball, the batter studies the pitcher to see if he will tip his next throw. In poker, each player knows that the game's outcome is not just dependent upon the cards; they look for "tells," changes in the body language or demeanor of other players that might provide a clue as to the strength or weakness of their hand. The coaching takeaway is this: when the things that can trip us up are on our radar, we are less susceptible to their negative effect. As Solomon said, "A prudent person sees trouble coming and ducks; a simpleton walks in blindly and is clobbered" (Proverbs 22:3 MSG).

In the game of life, another coaching principle that the coach must understand is that we are always vulnerable. As long as we are in the game, there will be opposition, forces that oppose our advancement. "That can't happen to me" is a sentiment that has proceeded the downfall of many individuals. Sadly, these losses could have been avoided had they installed a biblical defense system. We must raise our shield and never let it down.

Triggers

Christian coaches must be alert for the triggers, things to which we are susceptible and lead us awry. Scripture alerts us that God's Word isn't the only thing that is alive and active. Paul warns us that sin is busy working to distort our perspective as well:

> But once sin got its hands on the law code [God's Word] and decked itself out in all that finery, I was fooled, and fell for it. The very command that was supposed to guide me into life was cleverly used to trip me up, throwing me headlong. So sin was plenty alive, and I was stone dead. But the law code itself is God's good and common sense, each command sane and holy counsel (Romans 7:11-12 MSG).

This much I know for sure, if Paul can be fooled, then I certainly have got to keep my guard up! We must concentrate on God's voice as it speaks to us through His Word, so that we might drown out the clamor of this world and the other voices in our minds. We will never be completely immune from the attacks that lead to sin, but we can certainly minimize the risk of spread from this dangerous contaminant.

As Christian coaches, we should also realize that, sometimes, an adjustment is needed. Our Lord will make any modification that needs to be made (and He will not hesitate to enact the change). I have been on the receiving end of these lessons far too many times than I care to remember. Also, numerous times I have witnessed God intervening in the life of others to recalibrate their course and put them back on track. The Master Teacher knows the lessons we need that will continually point us to Him.

We have an instructor with a vested interest in our life's education, and subjugating our agenda for His is lesson one. It is counter to our culture to place anyone (or anything) in a position of priority over ourselves, and money is often used as a tutorial. One such example comes from an article authored by a self-made millionaire that I read not too long ago. In it, he advocated that the key step people should implement in their pursuit of wealth was to pay himself or herself first.[1] Yet, the Bible clearly says that we should "honor God with everything [we] own; give him the first and the best" (Proverbs 3:9 MSG). When we give generously to the Lord, before we do anything else, "Your barns will burst, your wine vats will brim over" (Proverbs 3:10 MSG).

Matters of stewardship are indicative of the internal struggle that is waged between our individual selves and our Lord, and if our course deviates from His directive, we can anticipate some redirection. It is a tug-of-war precipitated by external forces and human nature that promotes this division. The Holy Spirit strives to pull us up, but Ephesians (2:2-3) declares that there are three forces constantly trying to drag us down:

- "the ways of this world,"
- "the ruler of the kingdom of the air," and
- "the cravings of our flesh."

The world, the enemy, and the flesh. The attacks come from the outside, but they come from within as well. As long as we live in our earthly bodies, the battle will rage for lordship of our lives. After all, it was the attempted coup d'état in the Garden of Eden that drew the line in the sand between mankind and the Lord. Since that time, we have been in a perpetual fight with ourselves. We have sought to play God, assigned god-like responsibility to others (in hopes that they might meet our needs), and we have let God be God (our only hope for full restoration to our original state).

Our hope of victory does not rest in one's willpower or depend upon the efforts of others; it resides in a continual reliance on His providence and His presence. Our dependence on Him frees us to pursue His agenda over our own. Even then, we must remain alert and constantly self-assess the motives behind our actions (James 4:3). At any one moment, the Christian coach exists in one of only three possible states: God-centered, self-centered or re-centered. We must be cautious. If we are not careful, even self-centered intentions can be unconsciously veiled within godly goals. This occurs one of two ways: through possessiveness and self-absorption.

The Flesh: A Re-Centering Remedy

As a head football coach, I employed a "whole person development" approach in training our student athletes on and off the field physically, mentally, emotionally, and spiritually. To be well-balanced, our strategy centered on incorporating biblical principles in each area. We truly believed that the lessons we provided would not only help them become better athletes; it would also improve every area of their lives, and the benefits would extend well beyond the time that they were under our tutelage.

For years, my life verse had always been Proverbs 16:3: "Commit to the Lord whatever you do, and your plans will succeed" (NIV '84). Not only was this my verse, but as a head coach, I made it the key verse for our football program.

I thought I understood what the verse meant, but the prism in which I viewed this passage distorted my understanding and led me to an inaccurate conclusion. Up until that time, I had presumed the formula for a successful Christian life was:

Merit > Pleases God > Brings Blessing
(my action)   (fulfills my desire)

I believed I was focused, but inadvertently my vision was refracted by self-centeredness. Erroneously, I thought that if I controlled the input, then the output I wanted would be guaranteed. Unconsciously, I was attempting to coerce God into working for me. My thought process was the opposite of what it should have been. If I had I been familiar with an Abraham Lincoln quote that I would read years later, maybe I would have turned things around sooner. During the Civil War, when asked if God was on his side, the President replied, "Sir, my concern is not whether God is on our side; my greatest concern is to be on God's side, for God is always right."

I had confused my preferences for my purpose. When Christ said, "I came that they might have life abundantly," I interpreted that to mean that if I pleased Him, then He would give me the things I desired. David wrote, "Delight in the Lord, and he will give you the desires of your heart" (Psalm 37:4). I desired to become the head football coach at a major university. In that way, I would have a bigger stage in which to bring glory to God and more money to give toward advancing His kingdom. I even remember my wife and I decided that we would not increase our standard of living should I attain that position. Our plan was to continue to live at our current budgeted level of income and then give future increases in salary to charitable causes. As I look back on it, I wonder, was I trying to entice God to work on my behalf? I had admirable goals but questionable motives.

I was confident my dream job was coming. After all, I had just led our team to its first-ever winning season, conference championship, top 25 national ranking, and the second-longest winning streak in the country at the FCS level. Only Jim Harbaugh's University of San Diego team had won more consecutive games. His time had arrived; surely mine was on the way.

But my way of doing things was about to change. It wasn't about what I did for the Lord; it was about what He did for me. His job was to stake me, or so I thought, so that I could play the hand that would bring the largest jackpot. It was a closed loop system that I believed would generate a win-win scenario for both of us. I believe my intentions were good, but my theology was faulty.

Tirelessly, I would strain toward these objectives, while fully believing in the doctrine I professed. He wanted 100 percent devotion; a heart that was uncompromisingly His. And, He wanted to give me a peace that, up until that time, I had not yet realized.

Psalm 127:1-2 said it all: "Unless the Lord builds the house, the work of the builders is wasted. Unless the Lord protects a city, guarding it with sentries will do no good. It is useless for you to work so hard from early morning until late at night, anxiously working for food to eat; for God gives rest to his loved ones" (NLT).

The Lord wanted to get me off the treadmill that was wearing me out and indwell my heart with desires that originated from above.

Everything changed for me one December day at a convenience store in Long Beach, California. I was pumping gas into my rental car and was about to leave when two homeless individuals approached me seeking money. I was in a hurry to visit with a prospective student athlete and his parents, so I gave money to the store's attendant and left instructions that it was to be used for any non-alcoholic and non-tobacco products they wanted to purchase. Feeling that I had done my good deed for the day, I left for my appointment and later checked into a hotel for the night. What transpired later that evening would change my life forever.

In the middle of the night, I awoke and sensed I was receiving a message from the Lord. "Is that all you got?" echoed in my mind. "Is that the best you can do for Me? Is that all you can sacrifice?" Immediately, I knew that I had made my career the centerpiece of my life and that something needed to change.

I called my wife, told her of my experience, and discussed what action should be taken. My first thought was to resign my position, but when I spoke to my athletic director, Hank Small—a man I greatly respected and a mature believer himself—he cautioned me to not get ahead of God. Providentially, he was currently reading a book that addressed the very thing that I was contemplating. In *Point Man*, Steve Farrar[2] states that he had resigned his position, got ahead of God and, because of his impulsive decision, he spent three years in deep depression.

Sensing that the Holy Spirit had provided wise counsel through my boss, I continued in my current position, but what transpired in the hotel room that night began to transform my life. The Long Beach story was about sacrifice, but not of a vocation. It was about sacrificing the number one position. It was about substituting my agenda for His and earthly rewards for heavenly ones.

Undoubtedly, God is moving in our lives to bring about His agenda for all of us on earth, but "don't get ahead of the Master and jump to conclusions with your judgments before all the evidence is in. When he comes, he will bring out in the open and place in evidence all kinds of things we never even dreamed of—inner motives and purposes and prayers" (1 Corinthians 4:5 MSG).

Did you ever go to church and sense that the Lord was using the pastor to deliver a message directly aimed at you? Then you have received His evidence and can bear witness that was an instance when the Lord used the church to help facilitate your transformation.

Not long after meeting with my AD, I heard a pastor share: "Whom have I in heaven but you? And earth has nothing I desire besides you" (Psalm 73:25). Message sent; message received. I needed to make an adaptation to that which I had previously considered fundamental. Keeping the main thing as the main thing meant an eternal focus. It would be a couple of years before I would retire from the career I had known for thirty years, but the transition was well underway. I would need to be repurposed first. Like John the Baptist, I needed to shrink in order for Him to expand.

Methodically and prayerfully, I began to look at scriptural passages through a new lens and assimilated a new and improved formula, one where I would not be at the hub. I now understood what Paul meant when he said, "It is God who works in you to will and to act in order to fulfill his good purpose" (Philippians 2:13).

God intends to give us "the desires of [our] heart" (Psalm 37:4), but God also intends to install them there. Our lives are intended to be God-centered and Spirit-filled. My newly adopted life verse reflected this change of direction: "However, I consider my life worth nothing to me, if only I may finish the race and complete the task the Lord Jesus has given me—the task of testifying to the gospel of God's grace" (Acts 20:24 NIV '84).

Eventually, I changed careers, but I have never stopped coaching. I just know now who is working for whom. Together, the combined income of my wife and me still does not equal what I once made, but ironically, even though we tithed before, we give more away now. Yet, we have gained so much more. Thanks to a halftime adjustment prescribed one sleepless night in Long Beach, I got just what the doctor ordered and just the medicine I needed. It was a re-centering remedy to remind me of one crucial fundamental: it's about Christ.

The Enemy: What You See Is Not What You Get

Someone once said that tests build up, temptations tear down. But I do not believe that is entirely accurate. Temptations only tear down when we give in. They are just another form of tests, and although "he never tempts anyone" (James 1:13 NLT), the Lord allows this form of testing to accomplish His will in our lives. Under His watchful eye, tests are introduced, not to see us fail, but to show us how far we have come and to take us even further. Before Satan ever inflicted any harm on Job or his family, he had to request permission from the Lord. "'All right, you may test him,' the Lord said to Satan... So, Satan left the Lord's presence" (Job 1:12 NLT).

The enemy will always try to persuade us that he is in control, but this is just a flat-out lie advanced by "the father of lies" (John 8:44). Even when he attempted to tempt our Savior, he did so using a pseudo-truth. The devil showed Jesus all the kingdoms of the world and told Him, "I will give you all their authority and splendor; it has been given to me, and I can give it to anyone I want to. If you worship me, it will all be yours" (Luke 4:6-7). Satan is the originator of alternative facts and fake news. He has no authority but that which he is permitted. The truth is, "The earth is the Lord's, and everything in it. The world and all its people belong to him" (Psalm 24:1 NLT). Authority does not rest with Satan and it does not originate with him either. It comes from Him who is the Owner and the Originator—"the Alpha and the Omega, the First and the Last, the Beginning and the End" (Revelation 22:13). Proverbially speaking, "The buck stops here!" (Harry Truman)

The World: Crowd-Pleaser No More

The fundamental question we should ask ourselves appears in Galatians 1:10: "Am I now trying to win the approval of human beings, or of God? Or am I still trying to please people? If I were still trying to please people, I would not be a servant of Christ."

The crowd always clamors for attention, but sometimes we would be wise to just give them the illusion that we are listening.

When Pokey Allen was the head football coach at Portland State University, he employed novel promotional gimmicks in which to entice the community to attend games and support the team. One ploy he incorporated gave the fans in the stands the opportunity to play an interactive role in the game by allowing them to call one of the team's offensive plays. He had a simple method to carry out the idea. Inserted in each game program were one green and one blue sheet of paper. The green piece of paper represented the ground and its use meant the fan desired that a run play be called. Conversely, the blue paper would symbolize the sky and its usage informed the coach they wanted a pass play. At a predesignated point in the game, the fans were told to hold up the sheet of paper that would demonstrate their intention.

I asked his offensive coordinator at the time how Coach Allen decided which play to call. I mean, in a sea of blue and green, how would you determine the preference of the fans? He said it was easy—I thought it was brilliant. Coach Allen would walk slightly onto the playing field, turn and dramatically scan the crowd, give them a wink and a nod, then he would tell the offensive coordinator to call whatever play he wanted!

There is an old coaching axiom that says, "Those who listen to the crowd usually end up sitting next to them." We will never get the security for which we long by trying to appease the crowd; not for eternity and not even for our lifetime. Their commitment is a contract that can be breached at any time.

On the subject of lifetime commitments, Lou Holtz used to say that the definition of a lifetime contract for a coach was: "If you're ahead at the end of the third quarter, they'll let you finish the game." Our desire should be to please an Audience of One, not the fans in the stands. The book of Romans reaffirms that this is one indicator of a God-centered focus when it states that "a person with a changed heart seeks praise from God, not from people" (2:29 NLT). Paul further reinforces the fact when he says, "So whether we are here in this body or away from this body, our goal is to please him" (2 Corinthians 5:9 NLT).

There's No Such Thing as a Freelance Christian Coach

A Christian coach does not need an IRS 1099 form to record his self-employment earnings because he is not an independent contractor. Scripture makes it abundantly clear for whom he works when it says, "Christ's love controls us. Since we believe that Christ died for all, we also believe that we have all died to our old life. He died for everyone so that those who receive his new life will no longer live for themselves. Instead, they will live for Christ, who died and was raised for them" (2 Corinthians 5:14-15 NLT).

As these verses point out and as I frequently reminded my coaching staff, although others employ us, we work for the Lord.

For whom do we work? Whose approval do we seek? It is a question of motivation, and it reveals not only our priorities, but also our view of chain of command. The one to whom we report ultimately determines whether we have adequately carried out our duties. In the business world, it is common practice for employees to have an annual review to appraise their performance. Their supervisors will judge whether they have met the standard that was expected of them. A verse from Romans admonishes us to remember that, on Judgment Day, "each of us will give an account of ourselves to God" (14:12). Christian coaches have a fiduciary responsibility and a royal position.

Every once in a while, we should pause and remind ourselves of a very important fact: the one who signs our paycheck is not the one for whom we work. Neither is the endless stream of people who enter and exit our lives the audience we should desire to please. We simply cannot "[love] human praise more than praise from God" (John 12:43). Christian coaches work for the Lord and desire to please Him; it is the reason each of us has been selected for service and the only motivation we need.

Jesus says, "You did not choose me, but I chose you and appointed you so that you might go and bear fruit—fruit that will last—and so that whatever you ask in my name the Father will give you" (John 15:16). We shouldn't require a halftime adjustment to become re-centered; we must remain

God-centered. It is the fundamental focus for the facilitation of fruitful work. It is not just about for whom we work, but what is produced by our work. Christian coaches are constructed upward so that we might proceed outward and our primary job is to answer a call to transport!

11

BRACE FOR BATTLE

"The harder the battle, the sweeter the victory."
Les Brown

When Rev. Joseph Tson was arrested by soldiers of Romania's dictatorship, he knew he was facing the possibility of execution. The commander pulled a gun, put it to Joseph's head, and threatened, "The choice is easy. Deny Jesus or we pull the trigger."

Suddenly the Spirit of the Lord filled Joseph's whole being. "If you kill me today you will do me a great favor. All my sermons that were recorded will be in great demand because I will be a martyr for Christ. You will help me greatly to share my messages. You will also help me to go to my Lord quickly!"

The shocked officer lowered his gun. "You Christians are crazy!" The commander ordered the officers to take Joseph back home. The pastor wrote, "Never again did I fear what man can do to me. Never again did I fear to lose my life."[1]

"Fear not" is a command that is not only repeated 365 times throughout the Bible for dramatic effect, the edict brings reassurance. We have a daily reminder that the Lord of the universe cares enough about our personal dilemma to insert Himself into whatever the situation might be. And, just because we do not see God in our circumstances does not mean that He is not there.

Elisha's servant felt fear when the king of Aram sent a mighty force to capture the prophet. "'Don't be afraid,' the prophet answered. 'Those who are with us are more than those who are with them.' And Elisha prayed, 'Open his eyes, Lord, so that he may see.' Then the Lord opened the servant's eyes, and he looked and saw the hills full of horses and chariots of fire all around Elisha" (2 Kings 6:16-17).

If you are currently in a precarious place, rest assured you have not been forgotten; you are not alone and you never will be. If your back is against the wall, know that the Lord has your back and His Word backs it up. The command contains a promise, and we do not have to read between the lines; it is there in bold print: "The sun will not harm you by day, nor the moon by night" (Psalm 121:6), and neither can a bullet in the chamber of any gun. "The Lord himself goes before you and will be with you; he will never leave you nor forsake you" (Deuteronomy 31:8). Guaranteed!

Painful Purpose

For a Christ follower, pain and suffering have a purpose. We always grow more during times of trial than times of tranquility!

There is a reason for everything we experience, even in the hardships we face. The goal of adversity is our spiritual maturity (James 1:2-4). I love what A.W. Tozer once said: "It is doubtful whether God can bless a man greatly until he has hurt him deeply." I could not agree more. For a Christ follower, pain and suffering have a purpose. We always grow more during times of trial than times of tranquility!

There are only two types of pain we endure: God-ordained and self-inflicted. On more than one occasion, I have prayed that the Lord would protect me from myself. The pain from God-ordained tests subsides, but the effects from my personal assault on myself tend to endure.

In either case, the good news is that His favor is the umbrella that shields us from the seemingly torrential downpour of trouble in our lives and our repentance turns off the shower we have turned on ourselves. His blessing is the pot of gold at the end of the rainbow that follows what is really a brief cloudburst.

Coaches are usually more successful because, once upon a time, we also played the game. We have experienced the ups and downs from our own careers, and the lessons learned are usually the lessons we are best able to teach. And there's one lesson we've learned that we can confidently pass along: when we fall, we can count on the Lord to pick us up.

In any given year, we're going to have a minimum of three crises, but a crisis isn't necessarily bad; it's how we respond to the crisis that makes the difference. This is a fact of life, and a coach must train his team to respond in a positive manner when adversity strikes.

Similarly, our Master Coach also knows that we must be trained in trial to transform as He intends. Just as turnovers are inevitable in athletics, they're inescapable in life as well. The Lord either scripts a scenario in our lives, or He allows stressful situations to occur, to teach Christian coaches a valuable lesson: "For every child of God defeats this evil world, and we achieve this victory through our faith" (1 John 5:4 NLT). When our faith is tested, we find out that victory is assured!

Christian coaches need four things to successfully manage a crisis:

- A reliable operator's manual to follow
- A lesson to learn
- A partner to assist
- A timeless warranty.

A Reliable Operator's Manual to Follow

Athletes study the playbook from cover to cover because the contents provide the answers that will optimize their chances for success on game day. In the playbooks that I helped to write, I always made sure that I put the athlete in a position where they could best be successful. For every play they might be asked to execute, there were three components that were addressed. I call them the AAAs: Alignment, Assignment, and Adjustment. Regardless of the position they might play, they knew where to start, what to do, and, if the situation called for it, how to adjust.

For the Christian coach, our spiritual playbook serves as an operator's manual for a similar successful migration. Coaches do not consider the team's playbook to be a leisurely read; we expect team members to examine it thoroughly. Likewise, Christian coaches have a similar take regarding Scripture; it is an all-important operation manual for life's game field.

Isn't it refreshing to know that we have all the answers we need to life's most important questions in God's Word?! We don't need to do any more research on any of these topics. Solomon maintained, "There is no end to the publishing of books, and constant study wears you out so you're no good for anything else. The last and final word is this: Fear God. Do what he tells you" (Ecclesiastes 12:13 MSG). The application might be complicated, but the instruction is not complex. The Christian coach can carry out his assignment because they have documented evidence of the Lord's reliability and empathy.

When people know what to expect, they feel more secure. Consistency breeds dependability and lays a foundation of trust. The writer of Hebrews says, "Jesus Christ is the same yesterday and today and forever" (13:8). Based upon this fact, with absolute certainty we can predict how the book of Jay, Tim, Pam and (insert your name here) will end. Spoiler alert: it ends well for the fully devoted follower of Jesus Christ. So great is the story that is written for those He adores that we cannot fully comprehend what is coming next. He will unfold what awaits us as we turn the next page. Truly, "No eye has seen, no ear has heard, and no mind has imagined what God has prepared for those who love him" (1 Corinthians 2:9 NLT). In short, the Lord promises to meet all our needs—and then some!

We will not sink, and we will not lean; He will support us and keep us upright.

"And now to him who can keep you on your feet, standing tall in his bright presence, fresh and celebrating—to our one God, our only Savior, through Jesus Christ, our Master, be glory, majesty, strength, and rule before all time, and now, and to the end of all time. Yes" (Jude 1:24 MSG).

Who among us does not want a little empathy when we are in the midst of a difficulty? We receive comfort when we know that someone can relate, they have faced a similar trial, and they can reassure us by sharing their own comeback saga. No matter what you are going through, He understands. "For we do not have a high priest who is unable to empathize with our weaknesses, but we have one who has been tempted in every way, just as we are—yet he did not sin" (Hebrews 4:15). Jesus has walked a mile in our shoes; He personally experienced every up and down.

We can trust Christ to meet our needs. But we can't just read about it, we must experience it for ourselves. God has worked a plan of restoration to return our relationship with Him to its original state, one in which we once again place our full reliance upon Him. To live differently, coaches must think differently.

But we are not the first to receive this training; there is a procession that has preceded us. Never has His initiative been more evident than when the Israelites traveled through the wilderness on their way to the Promised Land. They were free from their oppressors, but still enslaved by their past. To alter the diet that had been "baked in" over 400 years, the Jewish nation would need to be introduced to a new menu.

A Lesson to Learn: Training Grounds Rest upon a Traveling Rock

Similar to a skillful surgeon, the Lord has a variety of instruments at His disposal with which He can operate. Discriminatingly, He selects the one that will surely get our undivided attention.

As His people departed Egypt and began their trek across the wilderness, the Lord initiated His operation by selecting a scalpel that would cut to the heart of one of their most basic physiological needs: the need for food and water (and it certainly got their attention). The Israelite people complained to Moses, "You have brought us out into this desert to starve this entire assembly to death."

They had everything they needed. "All of them ate the same spiritual food, and all of them drank the same spiritual water. For they drank from the spiritual rock that traveled with them, and that rock was Christ" (1 Corinthians 10:3–4 NLT).

Paul tells us that "if we have food and clothing, with these we will be content" (1 Timothy 6:8 ESV). And Paul practiced what he preached. But the Jewish community was not satisfied with the Lord's provision; they still wanted more. So, in answer to their grumbling, God provided quail to satisfy their want (Exodus 16:11-13 and Numbers 11:4-6; 31-33).

Paul expressed the proper attitude when he said, "I know what it is to be in need, and I know what it is to have plenty. I have learned the secret of being content in any and every situation, whether well fed or hungry, whether living in plenty or in want" (Philippians 4:12).

The apostle had learned to yield to God for his daily provision, but failure to learn the lesson of contentment had severe consequences for the Jewish nation. A plague of epidemic proportions beset the people and the infection was delivered through that which they craved—the quail. The meat that they coveted did not deliver the contentment they sought.

I wonder, "How many times have I selfishly expressed dissatisfaction with God's provision and how many times has He shown me mercy by not afflicting me by giving me the very thing that I asked?" Christian coaches should "think about the things of heaven, not the things of earth" (Colossians 3:2 NLT). We should choose provision over preference and remember to "do everything without grumbling" (Philippians 2:14). It is a lesson worth learning.

God created the need and then met it. And He will train us similarly. He'll deprive us of a need until we learn to turn to Him for its supply. There's no limit to the number of subject lessons at our Lord's disposal. Until we pass with flying colors, we can anticipate further testing.

The Lord can be trusted to meet our needs as we surrender ourselves daily to His service. Our inspection leads to this undeniable truth: the living water of Jesus Christ is always with us as we journey through this life. The rock upon which we rest is mobile because we carry Jesus with us wherever we go—transforming while transporting.

There is no matter too large or too insignificant that we cannot turn it over to the Great Physician. No matter the turbulence, He has both the method and the means upon which we can rely. As He skillfully operates in our lives to remove all doubt that He is able, aspiring coaches can nurture that same confidence in the VPs whom they transport. On matters of trust, we move forward each day in one of three states: Seclusion, Delusion, or Resolution.

We can choose to seclude ourselves and operate under the false notion that we can address all our needs. The second alternative is to delude ourselves into believing that others either will, or are required to, fulfill that role. Finally, we can come to the resolution that through Jesus Christ all our necessities will be met. Paul says we can live with 100 percent assurance that "my God will meet all your needs according to the riches of his glory in Christ Jesus" (Philippians 4:19).

A Partner to Assist

Christ followers must resist a tendency to isolate themselves during troubling times. We don't refresh ourselves by withdrawing; we connect to the Lord and we stay engaged with our brothers and sisters in Christ. As Solomon said, "Two people are better off than one, for they can help each other succeed. If one person falls, the other can reach out and help. But someone who falls alone is in real trouble. Likewise, two people lying close together can keep each other warm. But how can one be warm alone? A person standing alone can be attacked and defeated, but to can stand back-to-back and conquer. Three are even better, for a triple braided cord is not easily broken" (Ecclesiastes 4:9-12 NLT).

As Christ followers, we are on a journey, but it was never intended that we should go it alone. Relationships provide preventive maintenance that lessens the likelihood of breakdown, but if a malfunction does occur, they can also provide repair along our way. Christian coaches have teammates to help pick us up when we are down; it's a "Coaches Association."

Everyone is a VP to someone! As we lead others, we ourselves are also led. We are coaching while being coached ourselves. It's the Lord's parallel system to failsafe each other's spiritual walk. The

> *The process we undergo and the production we lead provide the progression we follow and the pathway we share! Together, we all move onward.*

process we undergo and the production we lead provide the progression we follow and the pathway we share! Together, we all move onward.

Others ⟶ Us ⟶ Others

There's an adage: if you see a turtle on a fence, you know it didn't get there itself—somebody put it there. We are where we are today because of someone else. We stand upon another's shoulders and we brace to support those who stand on ours. In any relationship, trust is elevated when the responsibility for the outcome is shared. Life is a team sport and only together is there victory. Thank God we do not have to go it alone! For the valued participant and the Christian coach there is always a person in the trenches with them.

A Timeless Warranty

Jesus decrees, "I am with you always" (Matthew 28:20), and the psalmist declares, "He remembers his covenant forever" (111:5). Because of the New Covenant, mediated in Christ Jesus, Christian coaches can be confident that their future is eternally secure. Jesus Himself stated that it was an undeniable fact: "I give them eternal life, and they shall never perish; no one will snatch them out of my hand" (John 10:28). The covenant ensures that we will have all we will ever need, and not just in eternity, but in the present as well.

His consistency through the circumstances of our lives will remove our fear and replace it with greater faith. Over and over again, Scripture echoes this assertion: Consistency breeds confidence; repetition reinforces reliability. "You are always the same; you will live forever" (Psalm 102:27 NLT). He cannot deny who He is; it is in His character. He is righteous and in His righteousness we can be confident that He will keep promises. For our protection, and provision we can depend on Him—always and forever.

12

HAVE SKIN IN THE GAME

"Words are from the lips, actions are from the heart."
Rashida Costa

In 1986 I had the privilege of working alongside Bob Gladieux on Lou Holtz's first coaching staff at the University of Notre Dame. As an alum, Bob Gladieux was already a well-recognized name among Fighting Irish fans. In the long succession of legendary performances of those who donned the Blue and Gold, Bob left his permanent mark on the timeline in Notre Dame's storied football history two decades earlier. In what was known as "the game of the century," Bob scored the tying touchdown for the number one–ranked Fighting Irish as they took on the second–ranked Michigan State Spartans. In so doing, he secured his place alongside other Fighting Irish gridiron greats.

As a rookie for the then Boston Patriots, Bob had a rather unique experience. In those days the American Football League was still a fledgling enterprise and a few years away from merging with the well-established National Football League, so they did whatever they could to reduce expenses. One such cost-saving measure led team management to cut some players from the roster just prior to the team's last exhibition game, so that they might have a skeletal crew for the remaining contest, and then to re-sign them when they were ready to begin the regular season. Bob was one of these individuals.

Having nothing else to do on this particular day, and because the last preseason game was hosted by the Patriots, Bob decided to attend the contest with one of his good friends. As the pregame warm-ups drew to a close, Bob's pal went to the concession stand to pick up refreshments for them both, while Bob remained behind.

What Bob and his friend did not know was that one of the Patriot players had injured himself during warm-ups and, like Bob, he also happened to be a running back. Because of the commotion under the stands, Bob's pal could not hear what Bob heard come over the public address system: "Would Bob Gladieux please report to the Patriots' locker room—Bob Gladieux." Having no idea why he was being paged (and reasoning that he would be back well before his friend returned from the concession line), Bob chose not to apprise his mate of the situation but, instead, dutifully made his way to the team's dressing room.

When Bob checked in he discovered his equipment and uniform waiting for him. The explanation he sought he never received, but his instructions were to the point: "Suit up." Still trying to comprehend what had just transpired, Bob quickly got dressed and headed for the Patriots' sideline.

Since the injured team member that Bob replaced was also on the kickoff coverage squad, Bob was placed in the position that had just been vacated and immediately guided onto the game field. Astonishingly, although he really had no idea what he was doing and he had not had so much as a chance to stretch (or even touch his toes!), Bob ran down the field and somehow stumbled into the Miami Dolphins' ball carrier. It was just at that precise moment that Bob's friend emerged from the concourse and made his way back to their seats carrying their drinks and snacks. He was curious about

Bob's absence, but even more puzzled when he heard from the loudspeaker: "Bob Gladieux on the tackle!"

When the Master Coach needs someone to go, coaches do not look around to see if another can fill the position. They gladly volunteer, step up, and proclaim, "Here am I. Send me" (Isaiah 6:8). Similar to Bob, Christian coaches never know when their number might be dialed, but when their time arrives, they never fail to answer the call. And, like Bob, they are ready to scramble in a moment's notice. To paraphrase Knute Rockne, "One man practicing faith is far better than 100 teaching it!"

Ready for Action

Christian coaches never clock out and Jesus tells us why: "My Father is always working, and so am I" (John 5:17 NLT). Since God is always active, we must follow suit; there's work for us to do while we are being constructed in the image of Jesus Christ. God is the foreman on the construction site and He's not looking for supervisors; He is in the market for laborers. Regardless of where you are on your spiritual journey—a novice or a seasoned veteran—Colossians states that the study of the Master will lead to our increased proficiency: "As you learn more and more how God works, you will learn how to do your work" (1:10 MSG).

It is about working smart, working well, and biblical principles show us how. The key then is to be obedient, and the biggest impediment to our obedience is us. A good work ethic is contrary to human nature and another example of something that is disavowed by the culture in which we live today.

There is a limitless supply of gadgets advertised whose sole purpose is to appeal to our proclivity to kick our feet up and relax. One of my favorite examples is the "twirling spaghetti fork." This battery-operated device rotates the fork so that spaghetti noodles effortlessly wrap around the utensil. Thank God! No longer do we have to exhaust ourselves by rotating our wrist! I don't know about you, but that manual task can leave me so exhausted that I am nearly unable to lift my arm so as to place the spaghetti in my mouth.

Amazingly, more than 2,000 years ago, Solomon described this very thing when he said, "A sluggard buries his hand in the dish; he is too lazy to bring it back to his mouth" (Proverbs 26:15). As absurd as some of these items might be, they would not be invented or sold if there was not a market for them. We all have to fight a natural tendency to be lazy and complacent, and we can do that successfully when we remember that the yoke is not entirely on our shoulders. When the Christian coach enters the game, he or she can depend on three things: the Lord above us, the Holy Spirit within us, and the team around us.

The Lord Above Us: He Does the Heavy Lifting

Saving faith enables a developing faith, which equips us to live out our faith. James asks a great introspective question: "What good is it, dear brothers and sisters, if you say you have faith but don't show it by your actions? Can that kind of faith save anyone?" (James 2:14 NLT). In other words, is that person even really saved?

Have you ever heard someone say, "Yeah, so-and-so is a believer, but they are just not currently practicing"? As believers, we belong to a team, the body of Christ. As a coach for more than thirty years, I can tell you something: that is an alibi that will not fly. If you were on one of my teams, you were going to practice or you were not going to be on the team.

Application is not optional; it is a requirement for team membership. Admirable intentions are all well and good, but our actions are what really count. John mentions that our actions not only verify team membership, but they produce additional benefits as well: "Dear children, let us not love with words or speech but with actions and in truth. This is how we know that we belong to the truth and how we set our hearts at rest in his presence" (1 John 3:18-19).

When we put His words into practice we will sense a level of peace that confirms that our game plan aligns with that of the Master Coach. Our humanity assures that we will not execute the game plan flawlessly, but the Lord is not looking for perfection. He is seeking loyal team members. Our obedience reflects a heart that is devoted to God, and our Lord can work with that. He will use imperfect coaches to deliver His perfect truth in love to His VPs. As Christ followers, we can be secure in our team membership when we have placed our trust in Jesus Christ and do what pleases Him. We are motivated to confidently tote that barge and lift that bale because the Lord will do the heavy lifting.

The Holy Spirit Within Us: Help Has Arrived

Growth of any living organism is either enhanced or inhibited based upon its skeletal structure. An adult human, for instance, has 206 bones. Without the framework provided by our spinal columns and the bones and cartilage that connect to it, we would literally be a hot mess. Likewise, our maturation is dependent upon the framework we allow the Holy Spirit to erect in our lives. The muscles of faith cannot be exercised unless they are attached to a spiritual vertebra.

Like Bob, if we just leave the stands and enter the field of play, Christian coaches can be confident that the Holy Spirit has a plan to do the rest. The Holy Spirit will:

- Direct Us—"For those who are led by the Spirit of God are the children of God" (Romans 8:14).

- Teach Us—"But you have received the Holy Spirit, and he lives within you, so you don't need anyone to teach you what is true. For the Spirit teaches you everything you need to know, and what he teaches is true" (1 John 2:27 NLT).
- Equip Us—"There are different kinds of spiritual gifts, but the same Spirit is the source of them all" (1 Corinthians 12:4 NLT).
- Intervene for Us—"Meanwhile, the moment we get tired in the waiting, God's Spirit is right alongside helping us along. If we don't know how to or what to pray, it doesn't matter. He does our praying in and for us" (Romans 8:26 MSG).
- Work for Us—"And when he comes, he will convict the world of its sin, and of God's righteousness, and of the coming judgment" (John 16:8 NLT).

The Holy Spirit undergirds the transformation of a Christian coach and inspires all the acts of faith that follow. Like the bones of our skeletal structure, the Holy Spirit permeates our entire infrastructure and reinforces the strength of the truth that originated our Christian faith.

Insider Information

The apostle Paul reveals the ultimate "insider information."

"But it was to us that God revealed these things by his Spirit. For his Spirit searches out everything and shows us God's deep secrets" (1 Corinthians 2:10 NLT).

"This message was kept secret for centuries and generations past, but now it has been revealed to God's people" (Colossians 1:26 NLT).

The meaning of Scripture was foreign to us when we were outsiders, but salvation gives us access to insider information.

The Holy Spirit unlocks what was once unknown and unveils the truth that was once out of view. Without interpretation, first impressions might lead to wrong impressions.

In 1982, I was honored to be named Illinois State University's Total Athlete. The award was sponsored by Athletes in Action (a subsidiary of Campus Crusade for Christ) and took into consideration academic and spiritual criteria, in addition to the athletic merit of the recipient. Thank goodness, because saying that my athletic performance was less than stellar would still be a gross understatement.

The featured speaker at the event, and the person from whom I would receive the award, was the legendary Archie Griffin. To this day, he is the only two-time winner of the prestigious Heisman Trophy. I was simultaneously humbled and thrilled to have him present me with my trophy.

Woody Hayes was the head coach at the Ohio State University during Archie Griffin's playing days. Growing up, I had witnessed Coach Hayes's tyrannical behavior on more than one occasion on television. Ultimately, his questionable sideline demeanor led to his firing after he punched an opposing player in a bowl game. Fully knowing what I would hear, but seeking to affirm my perception, I asked Mr. Griffin what it was like to play for Coach Hayes. To my surprise, he said that he loved Coach Hayes. He went on to describe a man who was selfless and truly cared for each and every one of his student athletes. Furthermore, he credited Coach Hayes for everything that he was able to accomplish on and off the field.

Archie Griffin had made me privy to information that was known to everyone on the inside, and it changed my perspective. It's a cliché to say "Don't judge a book by its cover," but the thing about clichés is that there is usually some element of truth behind them. As we live out our faith, we can do so with confidence, knowing that the Holy Spirit will guide us by unveiling all the pertinent information we require for the tasks that lie ahead.

The Team Around Us

Paul writes, "In the same way, even though we are many individuals, Christ makes us one body and individuals who are connected to each other" (Romans 12:5 GWT).

Coaches need a team; a consortium of like-minded individuals who share a mission, aka a church. A church is about both ministry and mission; it is a vehicle for both transformation and transportation. A church's ministry is to provide for the spiritual growth of its members. Ministry has an inward focus that concentrates on those within the church body, while mission speaks to outreach and has a goal of meeting the needs of others. The byproduct of ministry is the spiritual development of its members, whereas the addition of new members is often an outgrowth of mission. Together, they are the tools necessary for success in the coach-making business. A church is comprised of coaches, and its primary objectives must be to develop and produce more. Its purpose must remain relevant and that will only happen if we continue to fulfill our purpose and answer our calling.

Since the Fall, the Lord has used man in His restorative work. Although He is under no obligation to make us team members, He chooses to invite us to become His teammates in this venture. One of the many examples of man's inclusion in divine works of restoration occurred following the death of Lazarus. In a pivotal moment in His ministry, Jesus asked those who were with Him to "roll the stone aside" (John 11:39 NLT). Think about that for a moment. Do we really think that Jesus, who was about to bring a dead man back to life, needed someone's help to move the stone? Of course not. However, those who complied with His request that day had the privilege to participate in a miracle.

As Christian coaches, we have the same opportunity today. We choose to leave the sidelines and enter the field of play because that is where the action is. We are facilitated, so we can facilitate others. The church is the vehicle that transports valuable persons to the destination and coaches serve as both the beneficiary and the recipient of their service. Christian coaches are transformed to become catalysts in an impressive movement. The church drives the coach and the coach drives the VP.

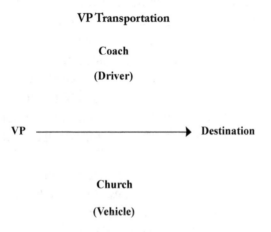

VP Transportation

Coach

(Driver)

VP ⟶ **Destination**

Church

(Vehicle)

Suit Up!

Years ago, an acquaintance of mine shared a story about an interaction he had with a famous sportscaster. At an event in Seattle, the keynote speaker was none other than Howard Cosell. If you were alive in the 1960s and 1970s and you had any interest in sports, then you would recognize Howard Cosell as the premier sportscaster of the era. At the conclusion of the function, the individual I knew approached the famous commentator and expressed his great admiration.

As he proceeded to ask for an autograph, Mr. Cosell asked the fan one question: "Son, do you have a ticket for this event?" My acquaintance was shocked, humbled, and a bit embarrassed, but his story provided me an illustration for this coaching principle: it's not your presence that establishes your legitimacy, you must "punch your ticket" to verify that you belong.

Authenticity is the antonym of feigning. Feigning is when we say one thing and do something else—it's hypocrisy. The Roman soldiers blatantly feigned submission when they "put a scarlet robe on him, and then twisted together a crown of thorns and set it on his head. They put a staff in his right hand. Then they knelt in front of him and mocked him. 'Hail, King of the Jews!' they said" (Matthew 27:28-29). The words of the soldiers contradicted their actions.

> *True submission and surrender are not just in the knowing, but in the doing.*

Words are important, but as Christian coaches, we need to remember that our words will be interpreted as disingenuous if not aligned with biblical application. Our actions either authenticate or discredit our testimony; they either help or hinder the leadership we provide. One of my former assistant coaches, Chuck Kelly, always used to tell the young men on our squad, "I can't hear what you're saying because your actions speak so loud." Coach Kelly understood that our walk must match our talk, and he consistently displayed it with each step that he took. James exhorts us to "not merely listen to the word and so deceive yourselves. Do what it says" (1:22). True submission and surrender are not just in the knowing, but in the doing.

I am not talking about a legalistic checklist. It's not by merit that we are saved; it is *by* grace alone *through* faith alone *in* Christ alone. Nevertheless, the words of Jesus should not be dismissed:

Knowing the correct password—saying "Master, Master," for instance—isn't going to get you anywhere with me. What is required is serious obedience— doing what my Father wills. I can see it now—at the Final Judgment thousands strutting up to me and saying, "Master, we preached the Message, we bashed the demons, our God-sponsored projects had everyone talking." And do you know what I am going to say? "You missed the boat....You're out of here" (Matthew 7:21-23 MSG).

Jesus is able to separate fact from fiction, imposters from those who truly belong. A friend of mine sent me a caricature this past Thanksgiving that amusingly summarizes this point. In it, a blind farmer was carrying an ax and walking around a pen full of turkeys. Multiple captions displayed that the turkeys were all saying one thing: "Moo!" Turkeys might be able to fool a blind farmer, but we will not be able to pull one over on our Lord. For a Christ follower, like a turkey, that is an argument that simply will not fly. He knows the real deal when He sees it (and hears it).

In the same way a uniform identifies an athletic team member, the Holy Spirit confirms our spot on the Lord's team. In Romans 8:16 we read, "For his Spirit joins with our spirit to affirm that we are God's children" (NLT). As team members, we don't just look the part; we play a part. To reaffirm what was previously mentioned, disciples bear fruit—good fruit. If not, the most eloquent of words will not be able to prove otherwise. "A tree is identified by its fruit. If a tree is good, its fruit will be good. If the tree is bad, its fruit will be bad" (Matthew 12:33 NLT).

Our Lord's words will challenge and give us incentive to produce good fruit: "Then Jesus turned to the Jews who had claimed to believe in him. 'If you stick with this, living out what I tell you, then you are my disciples for sure'" (John

8:31 MSG). We verify our position through our consistent and continuing pattern of submissive actions. Like oarsmen, we authenticate that we belong in the boat of the Master Coxswain by continuing to row. This is what we know: Christian coaches produce living fruit—disciples whose attitude authenticates what they acknowledge.

Action Steps

Here's what's true about truth: it is available, verifiable, and understandable for all.

When Peter proclaimed Christ as the Messiah, Jesus said, "You didn't get that answer out of books or from teachers. My Father in heaven, God himself, let you in on the secret of who I really am" (Matthew 16:17 MSG). Here's what's true about truth: it is available, verifiable, and understandable for all. The question is: what are we going to do with that information?

Amos 3:7 attests, "Surely the Sovereign Lord does nothing without revealing his plan to his servants the prophets." His plan is to use messengers (coaches) to deliver His message to those currently on the outside. While some environments are not conducive, even hostile to hearing the gospel message, we can still indirectly testify by implying our faith through our positive behavior and biblically inspired speech. When opportunities present themselves for a more direct approach, our voices should be amplified and our words must be precise. Implied or amplified, our faith is to be consistently applied. Whether implied over the course of his secular life

Implied or amplified, our faith is to be consistently applied.

or amplified through the conduct of his coaching activities, when it comes to acts of faith, the Christ follower "puts them into practice" (Luke 6:47).

13

SEEK THE REWARD

"Now may the God of peace—who brought up from the dead our Lord Jesus, the great Shepherd of the sheep, and ratified an eternal covenant with his blood—may he equip you with all you need for doing his will. May He produce in you, through the power of Jesus Christ, every good thing that is pleasing to him. All glory to him forever and ever! Amen."

Hebrews 13:20-21 NLT

I've always appreciated my brother Jeff's toughness. Because he is three years younger than I am, he fulfilled his role of aggravating me from time to time, and as Jeff's big brother, I dutifully fulfilled my role of tormenting him on more than one occasion. However, you can only push Jeff so far. I learned that lesson when my antics once resulted in him choosing to chase me down the street, while waving a board that had nails in it. Thankfully, I could outrun him.

Wisdom is being able to know the difference between when you should stand and fight and when you should flee! There's a fine line between courage and crazy, and for a brief period of time, Jeff didn't just put his toe across, he flat-out leapt across that proverbial line. I realize that I have taken a few calculated risks in my life (I ride a motorcycle, I have skydived, I have bungee jumped, and, most courageously,

I got married), but there's a reason why I have never been stung by a bee: I do my best to avoid them; I certainly do not confront them. If you mess with bees, you'll eventually get stung. Jeff's relationship with bees, however, is a different story.

At a very young age, Jeff had a date with destiny, and his saga centered around a conflict with these flying insects. An old garage on the farm where we lived would serve as Jeff's battlefield. The bees had claimed the garage as their home, and although our family really did not use this standalone facility, Jeff committed himself to ridding our property of its bee infestation. As Jeff saw it, it was an enemy invasion and he must liberate our territory from its uninvited occupants. The battle lines had been drawn.

Like a Roman gladiator, Jeff put on what he thought would be the impenetrable armor for his task: a youth football uniform. His battle gear was complete with a jersey, pants, and a toy helmet and shoulder pads. Jeff had alternate attire as well. When he didn't wear the football pants, he put on a pair of his Sears "Toughskins" jeans. I actually think that was a good choice. If you grew up in that era, you probably had at least one pair of these britches. Sears swore that kids would outgrow them before they would wear out and they were right because, when you don't want to wear them, they won't be "worn." The fabric was coarse, and the material so rigid, that I swear the jeans could stand upright even when you weren't wearing them. To me, those who wore them were more apt to walk like Frankenstein because their stiffness definitely inhibited one's ability to move.

Similar to a superhero donning his cape, when Jeff put on his uniform he was transformed into a larger-than-life action figure; he was—Jeff, the Bee Killer! With his chinstrap strapped and a flyswatter in hand, Jeff set out on his quest. The first couple of battles were won by this gallant boy; however, the war ended swiftly one day. A couple of bees got under his jersey and flew up his pant legs and the rest, as they say, is history. You reap what you sow is a proverb, and Jeff learned this painful lesson at a very early age.

The Biblical Principle of Sowing and Reaping

Coach Paul writes: "Work from the heart for your real Master, for God, confident that you'll get paid in full when you come into your inheritance" (Colossians 3:24 MSG).

The text not only instructs us to give our all in service to Him, but it also assures us "you will receive an inheritance from the Lord as a reward." As Christian coaches, we realize favor in this lifetime, and reward for the next, as we obediently work to accomplish God's agenda. When Christ speaks of giving us "a rich and satisfying life" (John 10:10 NLT), He meant immediately, the moment of our rebirth. The cross of Calvary is responsible for the grace that we receive—instantly and eternally. In response, we should possess grateful hearts that spur us to live righteously, for we know that the reward for such a living faith will not just be confined to us: "I was young and now I am old, yet I have never seen the righteous forsaken or their children begging bread" (Psalm 37:25).

There's definitely a lot at stake. Knowing this, one of my mentors, Paul Hansen, always emphasizes that "choices have consequences; decisions determine destiny." The impact stretches wider and goes further than we can imagine. It is the most basic of biblical principles to which Charles Stanley subscribes, "You reap what you sow, more than you sow, and later than you sow."[1] Broken down into its components, the phrase is more easily understood:

"You reap what you sow"—A farmer who sows wheat gets wheat, not some other crop. This is good news for those who are sowing good deeds, but this should be terrifying knowledge for those who live conversely.

"More than you sow"—The few seeds he plants produce a crop many times more than what he originally sowed.

"Later than you sow"—The harvest always comes later; sometimes much later than when the farmer planted the seed. For instance, some fruit trees can take up to seven years before they begin to produce any fruit.

Coaches, like parents, have the responsibility to pass along the biblical truth of sowing and reaping. Mallie Robinson, the mother of baseball's legendary Jackie Robinson, understood the importance of this biblical concept. Regularly, she told her children: "God watches what you do. You must reap what you sow, so sow well!" When it comes to sowing and reaping, Christian coaches should concentrate on worthy matters.

Inanimate Objects Lack Value

Life is about what we experience, rather than what we possess. The latter has term limits on its value; the former is of infinite worth. If Christian coaches are wise, they will sow to reap a reward that will not depreciate and coach others to do the same. Positions, objects, or money are not to be coveted. Possessions will tarnish, break, get lost, go out of style or fade from memory. Right now, as I scan my office, I see figurines on the bookcases for which I have no clue why they are there. They are ornaments that must have had sentimental meaning at one time, but my recollection of their worth is long gone.

Likewise, positions maintain no lasting value. Eventually, they will be handed to others when we exit them; they are the vapor that Solomon writes about in Ecclesiastes. Experiences, however, last forever. They are the things that led us to the possessions we acquired and the process that resulted in the positions that we attained. May they forever be etched in the consciousness of each one of us.

The Value of a Name

Experience does, however, tell us there is one possession that is worthy to be sought. In my college marketing class, my professor shared an interesting story that relates well. It is another lesson from another coach that has stood the test of time. Apparently, years earlier, a new line was introduced into the food industry with much fanfare and great expectations by a well-known manufacturer. In an era before microwave ovens, as the number of two-income homes in America grew, there became an increasing demand for meals that could be produced in a more expedient manner. This product appeared to be just what the doctor ordered. The prepackaged ingredients dramatically cut down food preparation time and, once they were combined with one pound of meat, in a matter of what seemed like moments, the dish could go from the cupboard to the dinner table. But, when the initial sales numbers of the item came in, the results were disappointing.

What made it even more confusing was the fact that the company's market research verified that, not only did consumers like the product's taste and preparation time, but they found it very affordable as well. Put simply, the product did everything they thought it would do and more! However, there was one thing they discovered consumers did not like: the name.

Originally, the product line was marketed under the name "New England Casseroles," and that is what they attributed to the lukewarm reception. When they branded the product, what the company had failed to realize was that the term "casserole" had a negative connotation. To consumers, the term meant the food item was cheap and lacked quality. When the product line was reintroduced under its new name, sales skyrocketed, so much so that the Food Network rated "Hamburger Helper" as one of the "Top Five Food Fads of the 1970s."[2]

General Mills only changed one thing: the name. It wasn't about the seasonings, sauces, or pasta that comprised the contents of each box of the hamburger supplement. It was all in the name. If a name is that important in a purchasing decision, imagine its significance in other contexts. Like "casserole," there is a reputation associated with certain names. Inferences are drawn from the labels ascribed to both objects and people, so it is important to protect our brand name. If this story tells us one thing, it is that a good name is, quite literally, a valuable commodity.

The one possession we should care about is our name. As a Christian coach, it will either advance or impede the life we build, the path we walk, and the message we are to deliver. Others will identify us by our fruit. It is the product a Christ follower reaps when they have sown good seeds. Our goal is to receive the recognition Paul credited to the Thessalonians when he said, "The word has gotten around. Your lives are echoing the Master's Word, not only in the provinces but all over the place. The news of your faith in God is out. We don't even have to say anything anymore—*you're* the message!" (1 Thessalonians 1:7-8 MSG). If we mean what we say, and say what we mean, it will become readily apparent to everyone.

One day—if it hasn't occurred already—your character will be attacked. It is not a matter of if, but when. On that day, people will examine your track record to determine the credibility of the claim. To withstand impact, your character must be attached to secure footings and built on a dependable foundation. If so, it will pass inspection from God and the scrutiny of others. Ultimately, it will confer upon us that which we have already established has infinite worth: a good name. I am convinced it is one of the reasons why Solomon wrote that "a good name is more desirable than great riches; to be esteemed is better than silver or gold" (Proverbs 22:1).

A finial dabra is a decorative object that is mounted at the pinnacle of a fixture. One example is the ornament that we place at the top of our Christmas tree. Metaphorically, a good name is the finial dabra that caps a distinguished life. It is the collectible that should be sought and the finish to the construction of a Christian coach.

A good name not only comes to our defense when we are under attack; it is also the means by which we engage influence. On any day, may those who listen to our words and watch our example take note of a lifetime's harvest of good fruit, and may our yield produce a plentiful crop of new disciples. What a great experience for us to collect!

You Can Take It (With You) and Leave It!

For a Christian coach, our worth is not credited based on a bank account; it is our character that truly counts and for which we will one day give an accounting. Coaches sow to reap a legacy that we leave and a reward we will achieve. The transformation process in a Christ follower is devoted to character development and the stakes are high. Our character is the only thing we take with us into eternity and its worth will be realized in the form of the eternal rewards.

But we aren't the only ones who will capitalize on a life constructed on integrity. When we sow a meaningful life, others stand to benefit as well. If we have nothing of earthly value to leave our loved ones, we can take comfort in the knowledge that our heirs will be entrusted with an endowment that will be impervious to marketplace fluctuation. Stocks and bonds might vary at the close of trading each day; material assets will depreciate over time, and landholdings are continually subject to the threat of recession, but a good name will only appreciate in value. It is a stock that is sure to rise and a collectible that is 100 percent recession proof. And even better, this lifetime investment can be transferred tax-free!

A legacy is born one day at a time. By consistently living a righteous life, we establish good habits and a high expectation that they will be repeated. In light of this evidence, people begin to view us favorably and grow accustomed to our manner, and a quality reputation is born. At the end of our journey may it be said that we were a living sacrifice that truly lived and may our descendants continue building on the legacy of our good name. Christian coaches get to take it with us and, simultaneously, leave it behind as well.

Compounding (Is in Our) Interest

Jesus said, "And everyone who has given up houses or brothers or sisters or father or mother or children or property, for my sake, will receive a hundred times as much in return and will inherit eternal life" (Matthew 19:29 NLT). John adds: "We all live off his generous bounty, gift after gift after gift" (John 1:16 MSG).

For Christ followers, eternal life is an inheritance—a gift that is bestowed at the moment of our surrender—but the perks we will receive will be accumulated through a lifetime of submission. Our birthright is guaranteed, but our bounty is contingent. We have absolute security through our salvation, but our reward is dependent upon our sacrifice and service. The question is really one of duration and vision. Should we live in the short term and for only that which is visible? Will we sow a harvest that will not last? The father of well-known author and motivational speaker John Maxwell provided a simple rule of thumb to help his son see the long-term impact of his decisions: "You can pay now and play later, or you can play now and pay later. But either way, you're going to pay."[3]

Christian coaches know it is better to pay the price up front than to suffer the consequences later. If we invest in eternal things, we will reap dividends that will never be exhausted. In Galatians, Paul elaborates: "Whoever sows to please their flesh...will reap destruction; whoever sows to please the Spirit...will reap eternal life (6:8). Moses "persevered because he saw him who is invisible... He regarded disgrace for the sake of Christ as of greater value than the treasures of Egypt" (Hebrews 11:27, 26). It was not the trappings of this world that Moses wanted to attain, but the reward of the next that he wished to claim. Moses was motivated not by what he saw, but by what he knew to be true.

As Christ followers, we should also focus on "Him who is invisible," as we strive to reach a higher standard. As Frank L. Gaines once said, "Only he who can see the invisible can do the impossible." Coaches are in it for the long haul. We may not see the fruit of our labor in this lifetime, but like a farmer who plants the seed, we know the harvest will arrive. Coaches pay it forward knowing that our residuals are coming.

"Let us not become weary in doing good, for at the proper time we will reap a harvest if we do not give up" (Galatians 6:9).

14

MAKE IT HAPPEN

"In baseball and in business, there are three types of people. Those who make it happen, those who watch it happen, and those who wonder what happened."

Tommy Lasorda

Christian coaches are not bystanders and they are not immune to the effects of their own actions. God uses coaches to transport individuals, and in that process, the coach is transported as well. Together, we cross the finish line (or, should I say, goal line).

At the conclusion of the final practice, before the first game of my ninth grade football season, our head football coach asked Don Castle and me to demonstrate how to use the two-man sled to the seventh and eighth grade team members. Even though we were not linemen (Don was a running back and I was a quarterback), the coach wanted to show his young pupils that to move the sled was not a matter of size, but of technique, effort, and coordination. The coach got on the sled and Don and I took him for a ride without much difficulty. After a brief pause, he upped the ante by asking a very large assistant coach to get on the sled with him. This time, Don and I struggled to push the sled across the practice field, but eventually we got the job done.

Like most teachable moments we experience in our lives, there is more than one lesson to be learned. Our coach successfully got his point across to the up-and-coming student athletes who watched our exhibition, but I learned an equally important lesson that day. It was one that the coach had not intended to include in his lesson plan, but an important one nonetheless: We all have something to add. We are either part of the effort or part of the resistance. Each of us must choose sides. We cannot push the sled and ride it at the same time.

One final lesson was also learned from this moment. It was that resistance might unintentionally inflict damage; the weight that we add can hurt others. That was certainly my experience. When I woke the next morning, the pain I felt was so excruciating I found myself unable to stand. Although the source of my suffering could not be pinpointed at that time, a few years later I had surgery to repair the cause of the inflammation I experienced that day. Needless to say, I missed the game that was held later that afternoon.

I want to be part of the solution, not part of the problem. I want to add momentum, not dead weight. Two are better than one but only if each person makes a positive contribution. If only one person pushes the two-man sled, the sled will go nowhere; it will only spin on its axis. I don't want to spend my life going around in circles; I want my legacy to be one of purposeful movement, not aimless inertia.

Like the two-man sled, my desire is to work alongside the VP and drive toward the goal line (and I am still committed to transporting whoever jumps on for a ride)! Don't sell yourself short; we all have something to add. You were designed to coach, and as a Christian coach you help, not hurt; you bring progress, not pain. Coaching is a transferable skill set, and Christian coaches are called to initiate the transfer.

Do the Math

Texas congressman Louie Gohmert warns us, "Relying on the Lord does not mean you lean on your shovel and pray for a hole."

The training process that constructs a Christian coach also propels progression in the production of new coaches. When Christian coaches choose to put their faith to work, they activate the belt in the manufacturing process that will move others. Our job is to add to the numbers as quickly as possible, so the discipleship wheels continue to churn.

In order to mass-produce, production must be accelerated. Output is always amplified through replication, and replication is a combination of standardization and multiplication. For output to increase, we need more people doing the work and more people striving to meet the standard.

Multiplying is accomplished through the addition of more people who are capable of perpetuating a skill set and through the addition of other team members, who in turn will contribute to the objective. Coaches produce coaches, who, in turn, produce more coaches. In Jesus' day they were known as disciples—coaches for Christ—and they began a very fruitful process.

Jesus said, "I am the vine; you are the branches. If you remain in me and I in you, you will bear much fruit; apart from me you can do nothing" (John 15:5). Only by remaining attached to the vine can we be fruitful, and only through the multiplication of coaches can coaches bear "much" fruit. Multiplication is a biblical principle the Lord has always used to fulfill His purposes.

It is a proven mathematical equation. Jesus Himself illustrated this principle when He fed the multitude (5,000) by multiplying the fish and loaves of bread. In fact, this event—and the concept that it demonstrates—is considered to be so important that it is the only one of Jesus' miracles recorded in all four Gospels (Matthew 14:13-21; Mark 6:31-44; Luke 9:12-17; John 6:1-14).

But the principle of multiplication did not originate in the New Testament. After the flood, the Lord instructed Noah to "be fruitful and multiply, and repopulate the earth" (Genesis 9:7 NLT). This directive remained in place until Jesus substituted it with a new objective for multiplication: "Therefore, go and make disciples of all the nations" (Matthew 28:19 NLT). What began as a command for procreation transitioned into a commission dedicated to the proliferation of Christ followers.

To maximize their yield, farmers, gardeners, and arborists look to horticulture for the most up-to-date instruction. Arborists study trees, vines, and other matters related to cultivation. They are experts in the grafting process, and they know how to successfully attach a new bud so that it will eventually form a new branch. Allegorically, VPs represent potential buds for our coaching tree. They are new disciples who will produce fruit and future buds to be attached to the vine of Jesus Christ. Arborists know what they are looking for in a bud. As coaches, we must recognize what a disciple looks like and teach them the truth so they might successfully bind themselves to the Living Branch.

A disciple reproduces Jesus Christ in himself so that, in turn, he can contribute to the replication process in others. It is what inspired Paul to tell all who would listen to "follow my example, as I follow the example of Christ" (1 Corinthians 11:1). Christian coaches know that what is good for the goose is good for the gander. Like Paul, we are to continue our training, so that we are more capable trainers. As Paul followed Christ, we should do the same. We attach ourselves to the only One who pulls us up and leads us on. As we progress, so do those who hitch themselves to our wagons.

Branching Out

"The disciples of John the Baptist told John about everything Jesus was doing. So John called for two of his disciples, and he sent them to the Lord to ask him, 'Are you the Messiah we've been expecting, or should we keep looking for someone else?'" (Luke 7:18-19 NLT).

In the coaching fraternity, there's a familiar term used to describe those to whom our wagons have been hitched. Coaches frequently refer to themselves as "disciples" of another coach. As these protégés are linked one to another, the interconnected relationships that form are described as "coaching trees." They are the branches of our past, present, and future. Personally, professionally, and spiritually, Christ followers are disciples that are limbs on multiple coaching trees. This certainly is true in my case.

I am a branch on a coaching tree. Personally, coaching has not just been my vocation; it has been a family business. My father coached junior high and high school sports for eighteen years, and without a doubt, he is the reason my brother and I entered the profession. One way or another, most of my extended family has served in some type of coaching capacity. Even my mom has identified herself as a coach, proving that you do not have to be devoted to athletics to be a coach; coaches come in many forms.

After unsuccessfully trying to enlist one of the coaching staff members from the high school teams to lead the Fellowship of Christian Athletes charter at the high school where she was employed, Mom assumed the mantle of responsibility herself. No longer did she call herself a music teacher; instead she referred to herself as the "Music Coach." For twelve years, she provided the leadership that left an eternal imprint on the lives of hundreds of young people and, in the process began her own coaching tree and one that continues its own expansive growth. It is not hard to be a

Christian coach. Like my mom, we just need to find a gap in which to stand and then be willing to stand there or look for where God is at work and be willing to go there. Willingness is truly the key.

You should have seen me fill in as the coach for my son's six-year-old soccer team. When his usual coach did not show up for the game that day, the parents elected me to serve in his stead. Somehow, they thought a college football coach qualified as an adequate replacement. They may have recast their vote, however, if they heard me ask their children an all-important first question: "Just how many of you are supposed to be on the field at one time?"

Professionally, I am also in a coaching tree. Some of the individuals I am connected with include well-known names such as Lou Holtz, Paul "Bear" Bryant, Woody Hayes, Nick Saban, Bill McCartney, Pete Carroll, and Don James. Others, although less recognizable, had a tremendous impact on my career as well. My fork in the coaching tree itself began its own tree. Some of the branches that extend from my tree include former assistants on my coaching staff who served under me, who are now head high school coaches, head college coaches, and assistants in the NFL.

There is still one greater tree from whom we extend. Second Timothy 2:2 states, "You have heard me teach things that have been confirmed by many reliable witnesses. Now teach these truths to other trustworthy people who will be able to pass them on to others" (NLT).

As believers, we have been grafted into the new covenant, established by the death, burial, and resurrection of our Lord and Savior, and into the responsibility to make disciples for Jesus Christ for the transformation of the world. He is the vine and we are the branches. Succinctly put, He is the Master Coach and we are His assistant coaches—members of His coaching tree.

Who are your disciples? Who are the valued persons in your life that will become part of your coaching tree? Like John the Baptist, our job is to produce more disciples, more coaches. It is a type of multilevel marketing scheme that will ultimately redeem a lost world. Our teammates (the universal church) began with 120 coaches gathered in the Upper Room for a prayer meeting and today has grown into the millions, but there is still work to do and "we're not about to throw up our hands and walk off the job" (2 Corinthians 4:1 MSG). Branches extend outward as Christian coaches transport their VPs through the four steps we'll discuss in later chapters: Engage, Escort, Equip, and Empower.

When we invest in the lives of others, our investment pays dividends that go beyond our time together, extends further than we thought possible, and benefits others in ways we never could have imagined.

Step Up to the Plate

As a teenager, Jack was heading down the wrong road. Although some of his arrests might have been attributed to racial profiling, a majority of the time it was due to his role as leader of the Pepper Street gang. Jack's mother was a woman of faith, and she had raised Jack to believe in God, but somewhere along the way he had taken a wrong turn.

Enter Karl Downs. Although he was only twenty-five years of age, in 1938 the young African American preacher became the senior pastor at Scott United Methodist Church in Pasadena, California. Reverend Downs set out to alter Jack's course, and in time his persistence paid off. This young Christian coach transported Jack back to the path that his mother had paved for him years before. As Jack's life was reconstructed, his influence began to build others up as well. Jack's gang built a youth center for Reverend Downs's church, and Jack not only attended, he became a Sunday school teacher as well.

Eventually, Jack left the neighborhood, but he never left his roots. Even while attending a nearby college, he returned every Sunday to teach his class. That is, until the Brooklyn Dodgers drafted him and made him the first African American player in Major League Baseball history.[1] Today, in his honor, Jackie Robinson's number is retired, not just by the team for whom he played, but by every major league team.

And to make sure that this milestone is never forgotten, baseball has set aside one day each year to commemorate the day that the racial walls came down. On April 15 (the anniversary of the day Jackie first took the field), baseball pays homage to the man who changed the face (and color) of the game. On "Jackie Robinson Day," I cannot help but think of Reverend Downs and wonder what God will do next if we surrender our lives and become one of his coaches.

In baseball and in life, it is always a question of who's up next. Who will be the next Karl Downs? Who will selflessly invest in the valuable persons in their neighborhood, and what might be potentially immortalized from such an investment? I doubt very much if Reverend Downs possibly could have fathomed the ramifications of his actions. In fact, I am quite sure he must have felt like he had failed to make contact on more than one occasion. However, unlike America's pastime, we always get credit for swinging away. Whatever we do in the Lord's name will not just receive annual recognition, but everlasting enshrinement. We might think we have struck out, flied out, or grounded out, but our life of service always produces a home run. We just need to enter the batter's box.

We Are Part of a Movement

Jackie Robinson wrote, "A life is not important except in the impact it has on other lives." Jackie Robinson did not circle the bases alone, just as Wilma Rudolph did not step to the top of the Olympic podium on her own; they were guided there by the loving support of others.

When Wilma hung up her track spikes, she did not leave track and field behind, and she did not forget what others had done on her behalf. She became a coach so she too could begin a process that brings about progress in others. As for Jackie, he became a prominent voice in the civil rights movement and its fight for equality. Life is about progress and the people that initiate the process. Present-day Christian coaches help construct future Christian coaches.

Scripture reminds us that we are not only built upon the Cornerstone, but also upon our predecessors. "Together, we are his house, built on the foundation of apostles and prophets" (Ephesians 2:19-20 NLT). These faithful saints encourage us to "keep [our] eyes on those who walk according to the example" (Philippians 3:17 ESV) they once set. They were, and continue to be, our coaches. The shoulders of those who came before us strengthen our resolve to provide support to those who follow. What we do today, and what we do tomorrow, is significant, not just for our time, but for all time. You and I might never reach the podium where we might receive an Olympic medal, but we can achieve an eternal victory and attain a heavenly crown by carrying the baton and running well in our leg of the relay. We must answer the call to transport.

"Listen! It's the voice of someone shouting, 'Clear the way through the wilderness for the Lord! Make a straight highway through the wasteland for our God!'" (Isaiah 40:3 NLT).

15

GET OFF TO A GREAT START

"Be generous with the different things God gave you, passing them around so all get in on it: if words, let it be God's words; if help, let it be God's hearty help. That way, God's bright presence will be evident in everything through Jesus, and he'll get all the credit as the One mighty in everything—encores to the end of time. Oh yes!"

1 Peter 4:10-11 MSG

It's an oxymoron to label someone as a disengaged coach; they simply do not exist. Coaches need someone to coach. They can only make a significant push by recruiting team members, so they plan accordingly. Christian coaches need to develop a plan to enlist disciples, and our recruiting strategy should include five components:

- Identify Viable Prospects
- Hit the Recruiting Trail
- State Your Case
- Keep Speaking Up
- Don't Underestimate Yourself

Identify Viable Prospects

College coaches use recruiting services to canvass the country in search of student athletes who possess both the academic and athletic credentials for success. They are willing to pay good money for this information because they seek qualities that are difficult to find. Coaches try to predict future performance based upon past performance, but an individual's previous accomplishments provide only limited data. The coach's job is difficult, not because of the information they have, but because of the information they lack. Each coach could benefit from a crystal ball, because they are predicting each person's potential for development.

The task is much easier for a Christian coach. We don't care about an individual's past; when they became a Christ follower they started anew. Christian coaches also do not need to project potential, because all believers have full access to the infinite power of God Almighty. They lack nothing. When it comes to initial engagement, there is an important coaching point Christian coaches understand: everyone is a viable prospect and their potential is unlimited.

The Bible establishes that we are of infinite worth when it says Christ died for everyone (2 Corinthians 5:15). Therefore, everyone the Lord puts in the Christian coach's path is a divine appointment and someone God valued enough to sacrifice His only Son. God is no respecter of persons. In case we do not understand, Scripture makes it crystal clear that there is no preferential or prejudicial treatment allocated when it states, "In Christ's family there can be no division into Jew and non-Jew, slave and free, male and female. Among us you are all equal" (Galatians 3:28 MSG). We are all of equal value, and we are all highly valued in His eyes.

Jesus Himself illustrates the infinite worth He assigns to us in the parable of the lost sheep. In the parable, Jesus responds to the criticism He receives from associating with those who have been labeled sinners by asking a simple question: "Suppose one of you has a hundred sheep and loses one of them. Doesn't he leave the ninety-nine in the open country and go after the lost sheep until he finds it?" (Luke 15:4).

His point is that God is nondiscriminatory. The lost sheep was not identified by name, but by need. We have value, not based upon who we are, but by Whose we are. Thus, the inference that can be made is that it did not matter who was lost; it only mattered that the lost was saved. They are the precious cargo we are to transport on our journey.

> *We have value, not based upon who we are, but by Whose we are. Thus, the inference that can be made is that it did not matter who was lost; it only mattered that the lost was saved.*

Jesus said, "Every plant that my heavenly Father has not planted will be pulled up by the roots" (Matthew 15:13), but Paul assured us that Jesus also "wants all people to be saved" (I Timothy 2:4). The fact that Christ has not yet returned is confirmation. Athletic coaches establish depth charts for their team, but not the Lord; on the Lord's squad, everyone is first team. Christ has made it a priority to go after every lost sheep, and He has devoted time for an extensive search. As Christ followers, we are to join the search party.

Hit the Recruiting Trail

Most men's Saturday morning breakfasts are poorly attended, but in many churches they are an expectation. I enjoy the breakfasts as much as anyone; however, strategically and objectively, are they still effective? The men who frequent these breakfasts look a lot like me—older and either empty-nesters or men whose children are self-sufficient. After an impartial examination of this men's ministry tool, one thing became evident to my former church's leadership: we were not reaching enough men, nor were we reaching the next generation.

Successful coaches alter their recruiting plan if it proves to be unproductive; if something is broke, they set out to fix it. Coaches must assess the results, and then, when the outcomes are unfavorable, they must look to their playbook and call another play. For a fruitful ministry, we must ask the right questions. In this instance, the question is not how we might increase attendance at the men's breakfast. The correct question is: how can we disciple more men? The question is not, how can we get them to come to us? It's where do we need to go to connect with them? In the three decades that I spent recruiting football prospects, never once did one fall into my lap.

Christian coaches need to meet them on their own turf; we always play away games. We hit the recruiting trail and go to them, instead of expecting them to come to us—no matter how excellent our activity might be. Whether it be in the secular world or within a faith-based organization, there is one key principle that is incorporated in every successful recruiting strategy: it's not about what they can do for us; it's what we can do for them!

It was at that juncture that church leadership determined that we must look toward other avenues in order to connect with more men. We needed to adapt our methods to build our market. The lesson for our church, our men's ministry, and all Christ followers is that Christian coaches must understand—and always remember—it's about people, not events. The message, not the methods.

State Your Case

"You have heard; now see all this; and will you not declare it?" (Isaiah 48:6 ESV)

All people have reliable and observable data with which to make an informed decision, and the data leads to an inevitable conclusion: God's Word is the source of absolute truth. "Nothing and no one is impervious to God's Word. We can't get away from it—no matter what" (Hebrews 4:13 MSG).

As Christian coaches, we might think the gospel message should be obvious and easily discernible, but we shouldn't assume that others already know—we need to put it right under their noses so they can't miss it. Coaches must present their case in order to determine who might be interested in joining their team. It's a pretty basic tenet in recruiting but is not limited to the athletic sphere. No products are sold, no services are rendered, and no association is formed without solicitation. Christian coaches must express themselves because they have a message that all need to hear.

Zig Ziglar once said, "You can have everything in life you want, if you will just help other people get what they want." Implicit in Mr. Ziglar's statement is the fact that every life is incomplete; all individuals lack something. Every item that has been successfully marketed incorporates this philosophy in their sales pitch. Whether individuals acknowledge it or not, Christian coaches offer one-stop shopping. Where else can they find every longing satisfied, question answered, and need fulfilled? Coaches just need to adapt their message so that it is situation specific.

Dr. Jeff Iorg, president of Gateway Seminary, says that there are four seasons in a person's life when they are most receptive to hearing the gospel: the death of a loved one, during a relationship struggle, when their health fails, and when things break (i.e., loss of a job). Christian coaches must be alert to these indicators so we can point those who are hurting to Christ.

At all times, however, our motives must be sincere. We should "do nothing out of selfish ambition or vain conceit. Rather, in humility value others above [ourselves], not looking to [our] own interests but each of you to the interests of others" (Philippians 2:3-4). We must take advantage of these opportunities to guide them to the Great Healer, while simultaneously extending empathy and encouragement. No doubt that will make a loving and enduring impression.

Christian coaches have the goods, but we must make it available to others. As someone once said, what good does it do if you discover a cure for cancer but keep it to yourself? When you save a life, you prolong someone's existence an indeterminable number of days, months, or years; when you save a soul, you prolong their blessing indefinitely. It would be negligent on our part, and a disservice to the Lord and to the prospect, if we keep the Good News to ourselves. Christ followers must be both consumers and distributors of God's Word. We must state our case and then…

Keep Speaking Up

"Do not be afraid; keep on speaking, do not be silent" (Acts 18:9).

Even if our testimony should speak for itself, Christian coaches don't let it. We verbalize it.

There are two primary ways in which coaches can speak up: we can repeat the message, and we can echo it as well.

Some people come to Christ immediately and dramatically, such as Paul did on the Damascus Road (Acts 9). However, for others the revelation doesn't happen overnight, like the gradual dawning that occurred for two men while they were walking on the Emmaus Road (Luke 24:13-35). Initially, they did not recognize that it was Jesus who was in their midst, but eventually His presence was made known. The coaching takeaway from this illustration is this: recruiting often takes time. The communiqué might need to be repeated.

When it comes to salvation, Christian coaches walk alongside their VP for as long as it takes. They may have been exposed to the salvation message in the past and even rejected it, but today's a new day. Regardless of the road that you are on, please know that you are making a meaningful contribution. You might "plant the seed" and another might "water it, but God has been making it grow" (1 Corinthians 3:6). You never know; your next interaction might just be the one that helps yield a new Christ follower.

Unless we live isolated on a desert island, there are a pool of prospects in our vicinity. We echo the message when it isn't just aimed at one person's ears, but it reverberates for all to hear. Coworkers, neighbors, relatives, and friends are present in each of our landscapes. They are the audience who must hear our voice; however, they serve as only our initial base of operation. Christian coaches, "'Go everywhere and announce the Message of God's good news to one and all'" (Mark 16:15 MSG). When it comes to the gospel, Christian coaches have the choice of either expressing it or suppressing it, but we should always anticipate that there will be those who try to distort or squelch what we say.

Understand Your Role

Once, when I interviewed for a position in the secular domain, I easily received more inquiry that day about my personal faith than questions related to my professional qualifications for the open position. Although the line of questioning was certainly illegal, it was still a window of opportunity that might remove the veil from the one to whom I was speaking. While engaged in a lengthy conversation centered on Christianity, I was simultaneously praying for wisdom in this discussion.

As I sought guidance, my foremost thought was, "How can I get this person to understand what I am saying?" Immediately, I sensed the answer: my job was not to convince; my job was to convey. I was to share what I knew to be true and leave comprehension to the Holy Spirit.

Dr. Wiersbe agrees: "Men can give us information, but only the Spirit can give us illumination and help us understand spiritual truths." What was true for me that day is true for all of us every day, but sometimes I think we get confused about the contents of our job description. We are to be His witnesses; to testify to that which He has done in our lives. It is not our job to change another person's heart because only God can accomplish that.

Our responsibility is to obediently express the gospel of God's grace to those He puts on our path. That's it; He will do the rest. For years, I didn't get it. Inaccurately, I thought that success or failure in scenarios such as this job interview were dependent upon my actions. When I shared the Good News, I thought if that person expressed a desire to profess Jesus Christ as their Lord and Savior, then I had been successful. However, if they did not make that decision, then I saw it as a failure on my part. Over time, I realized the error of my rationale—as the saying goes, you can lead a horse to water, but you cannot make him drink.

We are successful when we share the gospel, thereby unleashing the power of the Holy Spirit to present the opportunity to those within earshot to come to the saving place of understanding and capitulate their lives to Jesus Christ. How that person responds is between them and the Lord Almighty. We are only a failure if we are unwilling to faithfully execute our duties. As General Stonewall Jackson once said, "Duty is ours; consequences are God's." Usually, the platform on which we expound our testimony will be small and inconspicuous, but at other times the stage can be very grand and extremely visible. It can even make national news.

During the 2017 confirmation hearings,[1] an eye-opening exchange occurred between Vermont Senator Bernie Sanders and Russell Vought, the nominee for deputy director of the Office of Management and Budget. Although Article V2 of the US Constitution states that "no religious test shall ever be required as a qualification to any office or public trust under the United States," to many, Senator Sanders appeared to cross the line during his questioning of Mr. Vought.

As an alum of Wheaton College, Vought had written an article that supported the university's decision to dismiss Larycia Hawkins, a political science professor at the institution, over Facebook comments she had posted that expressed solidarity with Muslims. During the course of the hearing, Senator Sanders declared Vought to be Islamophobic and his nomination to be unacceptable. The passage from the year-old article that the senator referenced, and that he found most objectionable, was Vought's statement that "Muslims do not simply have a deficient theology. They do not know God because they have rejected Jesus Christ His Son, and they stand condemned."

In his response, Vought asserted, "As a Christian, I believe that all individuals are made in the image of God and are worthy of dignity and respect, regardless of their religious beliefs." He defended what he wrote by stating, "Christians believe that Jesus is the Son of God who is fully divine (and became fully human). If Christ is not God, He cannot be the necessary substitute on our behalf for the divine retribution that we deserve." In supporting Wheaton College's decision, he stated that the professor's comments created "serious theological confusion" about "what it means to be in relationship with or know the one, true God."

Although his nomination was delayed a number of months, nonetheless, Vought was eventually confirmed as the deputy director of the OMB. More importantly, he used a national forum to take a stand for Jesus Christ. At a pivotal time, without flinching, he shared John 3:18: "Whoever believes in him is not condemned, but whoever does not believe stands condemned already because they have not believed in the name of God's one and only Son."

It is because we love our fellow man and desire that they might be saved that we share the gospel of Jesus Christ. If we speak in any other way we do an injustice to society. That might mean that we might stand alone, like someone in a confirmation hearing, but, like Russell Vought, stand we must. Jesus said, "Whoever acknowledges me before men, I will also acknowledge him before my Father in heaven. But whoever disowns me before men, I will disown him before my Father in heaven" (Matthew 10:32-33 NIV '84). Christian coaches must speak up; there is too much at stake, both for those in our audience and us. We embrace our role, and then confidently move forward.

Don't "Un"-derestimate Yourself

Truly, we cannot go with God and stand still at the same time. We cannot say "yes" and "no" simultaneously. "Un" is a prefix that means "not." Its use normally denotes the opposite of what would be preferred and sometimes reminds us that the Lord works in unusual ways. Like in my version of the account of the woman at the well (John 4:1-42)…

Until the Samaritan woman had an unheard-of meeting with Jesus, she lived a life of uncertainty, but that was all about to be undone. She entered the exchange unwed, unapproved by the village, and, after one unusual encounter with Jesus, she unhesitatingly departed unburdened, unashamed, and unafraid to tell others about the unbelievable change she underwent. Once considered un-credible, her unwavering testimony unequivocally undergirded her message. Her story was unfathomable, yet the change was undeniable, so the still unsettled townspeople did the unthinkable and undertook the journey to meet the unknown Messiah. The results were unimaginable as He unlocked the unknown, unsaddled their burdens, and unwrapped their unrest. Unity with Christ was unexpectedly delivered through this unlikely vessel as history recorded the unforgettable story which unfolded, and the once unseen Savior of the universe now became unmistakably unveiled.

The coaching point from this story is clear: our voice needs to be heard; it is the volume in which the Lord manifests His message. Jesus said, "He who belongs to God hears what God says. The reason you do not hear is that you do not belong to God" (John 8:47 NIV '84). When her ears were opened, the Samaritan woman immediately began to coach. Her transformation led her to transport others to Christ.

If we are listening, we will not remain silent. Our silence could be deafening. As coaches, when we echo His words the Lord promises they will not fall on deaf ears: "So is my word that goes out from my mouth: it will not return to me empty, but will accomplish what I desire and achieve the purpose for which I sent it" (Isaiah 55:11).

But I am not done with "Un" (and neither is the Lord). The interaction recorded in John 4 provides a unique lesson: if you feel unworthy or unfit, you are not unique. If we are unwilling to act as God's voice, either because we underestimate our capability or His unmatched abilities, we unjustly deny the unchartered course the Lord wants us to travel. The Lord loves to use the "Uns" of the world: uneducated, unqualified, unknown. If you are one of these, you are in great company. Like the woman at the well, may we deny that we are unable, display an uncommon devotion, and carry out our mission undaunted. As you engage in recruiting, imagine what God can do through the "Un" in you—it could be unreal.

16

MAKE A GREAT FIRST AND LASTING IMPRESSION

"He who refreshes others will himself be refreshed."
Proverbs 11:25 NIV '84

I have been blessed to coach many fine young men over the span of a thirty-year career. Jake Heller was one of these individuals.

Like so many of the student athletes at Harvard—which doesn't offer athletic scholarships—Jake Heller needed some extra money. Most students chose work study, but Jake took one step further; he was enlisted in the Navy ROTC. I will always remember the name of one of his ROTC courses: Advanced Naval Weaponry Systems.

Jokingly, I asked him if he had to blow up some small island for a final. At the conclusion of that semester, I remember checking on Jake to see how he had done on that exam. He said, "I did great on the explosives section, but poorly on the targeting." What a great analogy for the awareness we must have as we examine our lives.

Targeting: Setting Our Sites Correctly

Life can be explosive, but as coaches, we must know that none of us will fully comprehend the target we hit with our conduct. For better or worse, we will each leave our mark.

In ministry, we often waste so much time trying to get people to stand in front of our target, when we should be targeting them. Our aim should be to find their "bull's-eye," their interests, so that we might be more accurate in our attempts to connect with them.

Ineffective means must be seen as deal breakers, but the ends are always nonnegotiable.

If our means are not achieving our ends, then we must be willing to change the means. After all, there is nothing sacred about the means. Ineffective means must be seen as deal breakers, but the ends are always nonnegotiable. To best connect with our VP, Christian coaches must hone our sights. As much as it is within our ability, coaches begin by removing barriers that might block communication with others. We adapt to the culture around us and work to establish common ground with those we engage.

Remove Barriers: "When the Walls Come Tumblin' Down"

Christian coaches don't meet a person halfway; they go the distance! It's not about what we prefer, it's about how we relate. In order to reach our communities for Jesus Christ, the coach's purpose must be flexible and rigid at the same time. We must be willing to "become all things to all people" (1 Corinthians 9:22), while holding fast and true matters of doctrine.

Our flexibility enables us to connect with the culture around us in a language that is common and acceptable, while providing a setting that is comfortable and familiar. The style in which we worship might—and probably should—be modified over time, but Scripture remains inerrant; its truth need not and must not be altered; it must simply be administered.

A compromise in its doctrine has dramatic consequences. Deuteronomy 4:2 warns: "Do not add to what I command you and do not subtract from it, but keep the commands of the Lord your God that I give you." In the same manner, when it comes to the fundamentals in a football contest or in the game of life, coaches need to be inflexible.

Football coaches know that losing possession of the ball will get you beat. As such, I simply did not tolerate turnovers; you might go so far as to call my intolerance to turnovers a conviction. Interestingly, the word "tolerance" is not found in the Bible, but the word "conviction" is.

The writer of Hebrews promises, "We have come to share in Christ, if indeed we hold our original conviction firmly to the very end" (3:14). When it comes to maintaining scriptural integrity, Christ followers are either men and women of conviction or compromise; there is no in between. If we stay true to what we profess, we can count on one day sharing in all that belongs to Christ.

> When it comes to maintaining scriptural integrity, Christ followers are either men and women of conviction or compromise; there is no in between.

Our goal is to deliver the Word of God intact in absolute terms; this is a matter of victory or defeat; life or death. Therefore, rigidity and flexibility are both needed for a church and a coach to remain purposeful today and in the future. Individually, our convictions rather than our preferences determine whether we continue to fulfill our purpose and answer our calling.

Establish Common Ground

Figuratively and literally, the closer the coach is to the VP, the better he or she is able to relay a message successfully. We tailor our message for our audience. There is no elevator speech; one size does not fit all. We show respect to the individual with whom we are speaking when we personalize our engagement. Christian coaches should work to establish common ground with the VP.

As we strike up a conversation, if we struggle to find an area in which we have a mutual interest, then a Christian coach should make it a priority to elevate the other individual by prioritizing his or her interest over their own. Coaches should "practice playing second fiddle" (Romans 12:10 MSG).

My father was outstanding in this department. He would initiate a conversation based upon the interest of the other person and, as a pastor friend told me after my dad passed away, if he didn't know much about the subject, he would study up on it before he saw that person again.

Coaches work to remove cultural barriers that might inhibit our interactions and we strive to establish common ground, so that our relationship with our VP might get off to a great start.

Names Matter: It's Up Close and Personal

Knowingly and unknowingly, we assign value to those with whom we interact, but there is a standard set for us. As Christ followers, Jesus told us that the second greatest commandment is that we love others as much as we love ourselves (Matthew 22:39). Human nature tends to lead us to classify some relationships as more cherished than others, such as those with family and close friends, but that does not diminish the important role Christian coaches play with everyone they encounter. Whatever their status or ranking in our lives, there are verbal and nonverbal cues that we can transmit to let others know that theirs is a relationship we value as well.

Theodore Roosevelt provided an adage that has stood the test of time: "People don't care how much you know until they know how much you care." One of the simplest, but maybe one of the most important ways that Christian coaches can show others that we value our relationship with them is to honor their name.

To me, it's very difficult to tell someone that you care about them if you don't enunciate and spell their name correctly. I have been frequently reminded of this fact.

Not long ago, at a church where I served as one of the pastors, a young woman told me that her family decided to become members of the church simply because I remembered the name of their youngest child. Since we are made in God's image, it is only natural for us to desire to remember another person's name. It's in our DNA, because it's in His character. Isaiah 49:1 proclaims: "The Lord called me from the womb, from the body of my mother he named my name" (ESV).

The God of the universe knows our name. It is just one of the ways we know that He values our relationship. You and I will continue to have memory lapses, but Christian coaches must continue to do their best to recall the names of those we meet.

It's What We Say and What We Don't Say

In addition to name recognition, there are other ways we can communicate worth to those we engage. For one thing, we can learn their vernacular, the terms they use and consider standard in their operations. For professional athletes this is common practice. Whenever they change teams, they learn the nomenclature of the new squad. It is only common sense that one person alter his or her language instead of an entire team, but I have seen individuals selfishly insist that the organization translate on their "terms."

As Christ followers, we all operate from the same playbook, so we should share a common language. However, when we first interact with our VP, we should not assume they speak our language. If it's important enough to be written down, such as Scripture, then it's important enough to be shared. Don't just assume they will read it; like Philip's interaction with the Ethiopian eunuch (Acts 8:26–40), read it with them and help them understand the terms.

Nonverbally, coaches can convey value as well. In the past, a firm handshake has been one important manner whereby we have communicated this distinction. However, the impact of the coronavirus on our society may limit this greeting in the future. If so, there are other methods we can utilize to let people know they are important to us. Scripture specifically points to our ears, mouth, face, feet, and hands.

With our ears and our mouths, coaches should "be quick to hear, slow to speak" (James 1:19 ESV). If God can note Cain's anger by the expression on his face (Genesis 4:5-6), then we should be mindful of what we convey by our facial expression as well.

Finally, if coaches want to communicate that we value a relationship, our actions must also prove we are worthy of that association; we must be aware of indicators that might prove otherwise. "A worthless person...winks with his eyes, signals with his feet, points with his finger" (Proverbs 6:12-13 ESV). The Message says they "cross their fingers behind their backs."

It may sound trivial but, whenever possible, I think about my feet, hands, and face, and I consciously incorporate techniques so my body language reinforces the message I want to convey: you are important to me. I square up to the individual with whom I'm speaking. I do not put my hands in my pockets; I put them by my side or cross them in front of me. And I try to smile.

If I'm in my office and someone comes to speak with me, I put my pen down and I turn my cell phone off. And I lean forward when they share important information. Visibly, I want them to see that they are a priority and that I'm focused on what they have to say. In all our communication, "Let everything you say [and don't say] be good and helpful, so that your words will be an encouragement to those who hear them" (Ephesians 4:29 NLT).

Establish Credibility

Early in the relationship, it's important to collect as much low-hanging fruit as possible. The reason is simple: it expends minimal energy, and it is effective in establishing your credibility as a coach. Some examples include the verbal and nonverbal methods of expression previously discussed.

Implicit in the term "two-way communication" is an understanding that more than one party is responsible for a successful connection. As the quarterback of the Lord's team, Christian coaches deliver the message. The receiver must be open to receive what is delivered, but the quarterback bears the greater portion of the responsibility for the completion.

For transmission to be successful, those we disciple must not only have confidence in the message but also in the messenger. The message must be relevant, but the sender of the message must also be perceived as a trusted source. In short, they must know what they are talking about. Only a fool would seek advice from someone they perceived to be incompetent.

There is a difference between thinking and knowing. It boils down to an assessment of probability. Whereas thinking predicts various degrees of probability, knowing means absolute assurance. Christian coaches know upon Whom and what we can fully depend, so we must act in a manner that supports that contention. On the way to a championship, a quarterback will experience many peaks and valleys throughout the season. Without faith, a quarterback will lack the confidence that will enable him to lead his team to the title.

Take Joe Namath, for example. Before Super Bowl III, he did the unthinkable: he guaranteed the New York Jets would defeat the heavily favored Baltimore Colts. Under his guidance, and as improbable as it was, Joe Namath led his team to a 16–7 win in what many consider one of the biggest upsets in American sports history.

Like a great quarterback, a Christ follower, and those whom they lead, can be confident in the final score. John guarantees that we will "achieve this victory through our faith" (1 John 5:4 NLT). A coach must be confident for the disciple to trust the message. If we fail to trust in the Lord, and in that which He is assembling in us, we will be incapable of leading our VPs to ultimate victory on the tenuous game field of life.

In everything we do, "there should be a consistency that runs through us all. For Jesus doesn't change—yesterday, today, tomorrow, he's always totally himself (Hebrews 13:8 MSG). Regardless of what the future might hold, He will "see to it that everything works out for the best" (Isaiah 54:17 MSG). This is the reliable message that inspires confidence in our future. On or off the gridiron, the Lord delivers His triumphant message through faithful messengers. When Christian coaches successfully engage with others, we can begin to lead them on the discipleship pathway.

17

LEAD THE WAY

"Go stand at the crossroads and look around. Ask for directions to the old road, the tried-and-true road. Then take it. Discover the right route for your souls. But they said, 'Nothing doing. We aren't going that way.'"

Jeremiah 6:16 MSG

Strategically, the Lord lines the channels of our journeys with valuable persons with whom we might enjoy purposeful passage. Whether they are a person with whom we are close or a casual acquaintance, there is a reason our paths have crossed and significance in our every exchange. We are temporary commuters on this earth, but we were never meant to travel alone.

God uses the coach to invite the VP to go along for the ride, to let go of agendas and embrace a better way, a higher calling, and a superior intellect.

"'For my thoughts are not your thoughts, neither are your ways my ways,' declares the Lord. 'As the heavens are higher than the earth, so are my ways higher than your ways and my thoughts than your thoughts" (Isaiah 55:8-9).

The thoughts and ways of God are foreign to the nature of men, yet they assure our arrival at the optimal port. Coaches are to look after their VPs' best interests even when they have lost sight of their goal. Former longtime Dallas

Cowboy Head Football Coach Tom Landry said it best: "A coach is someone who tells you what you don't want to hear, who has you see what you don't want to see, so you can be who you have always known you could be."

Those we encounter may not be "going that way," but Christian coaches supply the Power they need to propel them there nonetheless. We do not stand on the shore as they continue to go adrift; we go in the water to help.

Wade Right In

I like how Eugene Peterson paraphrases Romans 15:1-3:

> Those of us who are strong and able in the faith need to step in and lend a hand to those who falter, and not just to do what is most convenient for us. Strength is for service, not status. Each of us needs to look after the good of the people around us, asking ourselves, "How can I help?" That's exactly what Jesus did. He didn't make it easy for Himself by avoiding people's struggles, but waded right in and helped out.

When I read the words "waded right in" from the verse above, I can't help but think about the experience I had at my folks' place a few years back. I have always enjoyed speeding around the lake on a WaveRunner, and on this particular day one of my sons joined me. Hurriedly, we got dressed, ate our breakfast, and sped out the door. With each step we took toward the nearby dock our level of excitement and anticipation grew.

We untied the WaveRunner, pushed away from the dock, and turned the key in the ignition. Nothing happened. After a few moments of attempting to correct the malfunction, two things became readily apparent. First, our limited knowledge of this watercraft would make any additional attempt at repair fruitless. Second, without power, we had begun drifting away from the dock—the place to which we desired to return. Despite our efforts to rectify this issue, we floated further and further away.

It was then that it hit me: a rudderless boat rarely drifts where you want it to go. I had heard these words once before, but now they had relevance. The same

> *We don't drift toward excellence; we don't drift toward anything of significance.*

thing can be said for when we are on dry land. Without intentionality, we have little chance of reaching our goal. We don't drift toward excellence; we don't drift toward anything of significance. We only continue drifting away.

In my seven years on the coaching staff at Harvard University, I spent the majority of the time serving as the recruiting coordinator for the football program. You might be surprised to learn that there are approximately 15,000 high schools in the United States that have interscholastic football programs, and at Harvard, we made it a point to communicate with them all. After seven years of contact with literally thousands of prospective student athletes and their parents, one thing became perfectly clear: the ones who were eventually admitted to Harvard did not get there by accident. They didn't drift into Harvard—they were guided there.

Christian Coaches Provide Direction

Dan Chambliss, author of a study of competitive swimmers titled *The Mundanity of Excellence*,[1] stated categorically that it was not anatomy, but the manner in which they were coached that deterred the development of those who dove in the water.

Time and time again, I have seen comparable student athletes, in the classroom or on the gridiron, flourish or flounder, and the only perceivable variable is the manner in which they were coached. Scholastically, logic would tell us if we incorporated the same material in the same course, and the aptitude, attitude, and effort of the valued person remained constant, then we would anticipate a similar result. The fact that there is a variance supports the proposition that comprehension is affected by the manner in which the curriculum is presented. Coaches make a difference. Christian coaches make all the difference in this world—and in our disciple's pursuit of the next. Regardless of the activity, good coaches advance those under their care.

Christian coaches are exceptional and they are the exception. They are exceptional because of the potential impact they have in the life of the valued person, and they are exceptional because of the way in which they were assigned to this all-important position. There are no chance encounters; it is God who has orchestrated events so that our lives might meaningfully intersect the lives of others. The eyes of Christ followers have been opened, so we will not blindly lead others in the wrong direction. Our coaching tenure may be lengthy or brief; nevertheless, the interval is significant.

Christian coaches are the exception rather than the rule, because they are relatively few in supply. Jesus told His disciples, "The harvest is plentiful but the workers are few" (Matthew 9:37). There is no shortage in the number of people who need coaches; the opportunities to be impactful are boundless. We need more coaches in order to recruit new team members and introduce them to the privileges of team membership. We are the rudder the Holy Spirit steers so our VPs do not drift away.

Where Coaches Lead, People Follow

In the time of Joshua, the rules for discerning the Lord's directives were very specific. Only priests were allowed to intercede on behalf of the Jewish people. They were the only ones who could present offerings and sacrifices to the Lord, and only they could enter the tabernacle and approach the altar. More detailed still was the position of the high priest. He was the lone person who could enter the inner room of the Temple known as the Holy of Holies, and then only annually, on the Day of Atonement. During this ritual, the high priest would sprinkle blood on the Ark of the Covenant (the mercy seat of God), in order to cleanse himself and the Jewish people from the sins they had committed in the past year.

Now no barriers exist between a believer and God: "There is one God and one mediator between God and mankind, the man Christ Jesus" (1 Timothy 2:5). Not only is Jesus the mediator, but Hebrews 4:14 tells us that he has assumed the role of the "great high priest." Because of Christ's sacrifice at Calvary, we can confidently state that all our sins—past, present, and future—have been forgiven, and we have the privilege to enter His presence at any time.

Since the time of our spiritual heritage, there has been a modification in the clerical roles for those who proclaim Christ as their King. We "are a chosen people, a royal priesthood, a holy nation, God's special possession" (1 Peter 2:9). While the Levitical priests were called to lead the people across the Jordan River and into the Promised Land, in our time in history, we are a priesthood of believers assigned by our Great High Priest to an equally important crusade. We have been given the honorable task, through the Holy Spirit, to lead others through the river of life to the eternal Promised Land.

In the days of the Levitical priests, the tabernacle was mobile, and mobile it is still. In his first letter to the church in Corinth, Paul explains, "Do you not know that your bodies are temples of the Holy Spirit, who is in you, whom you have received from God?" (1 Corinthians 6:19). Yesterday, the priests' position qualified them to carry the Ark of the Covenant. Today, the Holy Spirit's presence within us qualifies us to be the vehicle to transport others.

A meandering stream transports water on a course that is altered over its life cycle. As the water migrates downstream, it erodes the outer banks of the river, while simultaneously depositing sediment in the opposite direction. Over time, this dual action produces a centrifugal force that modifies the flow of the body of water to produce a more direct route to the mouth of the river. These forces of nature work to channel the energy of the stream, so that a greater volume of water might be distributed to its destination, and its arrival might be accelerated.

While the Lord does not meander, He has altered our course so that we can more efficiently transport a greater number of VPs to their destination. Since He is in us and we are in Him, Christ is with us each step of our journey. When we move, God moves and when God moves, people follow. We must not forget that. The Israelites were told to follow those who carried the Ark. Now we are at the forefront. The God of angel armies is leading, and we, in turn, courageously lead our troops and go where God guides, because we are thoroughly protected. Hail to our Commander in Chief!

Give In, Give Out, or Give Them

President Calvin Coolidge wrote, "No person was ever honored for what he received. Honor has been the reward for what he gave." Each of us has something to give. Indirectly, coaches lead by example. Directly, coaches lead from the front. In both cases, we show others the way—and we courageously escort them there.

On the highway to heaven, Christian coaches can successfully guide others, if we continue to yield to guidance ourselves. Although it is not by chance that we are on the road we travel, we struggle with giving our control to the One who guides our feet each step on the path.

We are all control freaks. We act as if the priority of our lives is to insulate ourselves so that there is minimal discomfort on our journey, but it is this attitude that actually infects and compromises our spiritual well-being. The Great Physician knows that the only antidote for such a mindset is to take us somewhere beyond our control. If Peter, the rock upon which Christ built His church (Matthew 16:18), would experience this firsthand, does it not make sense that our Savior would lead us on a similar journey? Jesus reminds us it is only then that we can truly learn to rely on Him.

Someone once said, "God wants us to be where He wants us to be more than we want to be where He wants us to be." The process the Lord took us through in order to prepare us to become coaches continues on each leg of our expedition. This training brings progress and benefits, but it was never part of the grand design that the benefits we receive were to be used solely for our personal gain. Christian coaches are trained so that we might train others in what to attempt and what to avoid. When we go, we must make the most of it.

Certainly good coaches know what the Master Coach knows: most games are lost rather than won. To win, coaches must weed out the things that might cause loss. Similarly, the Lord uses a defect elimination strategy to refine us and He ingrains these lessons in us through a chafing exercise. Sifting is a process of separation with which all Christ followers are familiar. Christian coaches are sifted for a season and we are sifted for a reason; we are sifted for His service. Jesus impresses this upon Peter when He tells him that Satan has been given permission to sift him. "Simon, I've prayed for you in particular that you not give in or give out. When you have come through the time of testing, turn to your companions and give them a fresh start" (Luke 22:31 MSG).

> *Our period of testing is not designed to see us give in or give out, but so that we might give more.*

I get the concept of "sifting." You see, as a Christ follower, it is not just our reputations at stake— it's His reputation as well. Sifting is an important transformational process. It affords others the opportunity to see more of Him and less of us; it helps communicate the right message. Our period of testing is not designed to see us give in or give out, but so that we might give more. The Lord initiates this action to remove the impurities: the things that would effect a negative outcome. To lead others, we must exemplify the traits that are desirable to be replicated.

Coaches Lead Courageously: "No Guts, No Glory (for the Lord)!"

Jerry Seinfeld once said studies showed that public speaking was the top fear on everyone's list. The survey further concluded that death was the second most common fear. So, the famous comedian humorously deduced: "That means that if you're at a funeral, you'd rather be the person in the casket than the person giving the eulogy!"

Courage has to start somewhere and with someone. Somebody first hang-glided, skydived, and ate an oyster. As Robert F. Kennedy famously said, "Some men see things as they are and ask why. I dream of things that never were and ask why not." There's a cost for activity, but the price of inactivity is often far steeper. The first one through the barricade might get bloody, but if they don't go first, others will not be able to advance. Three times in the first chapter of the book of Joshua, the Lord told this great leader to "be strong and courageous" (vv. 6, 7, 9). The Israelites might still be wandering in the desert had he not courageously answered the call.

Willie McLaurin described courageous leadership this way: "Leadership is more than just a moment; it must be a movement. The difference between a moment and a movement is sacrifice. We must all be willing to make the sacrifice for a brighter future. To lead is to speak truth to power—and, as Christians, we have the truth. The teachings of the Bible are countercultural to our society. Thus, we must be willing to lead with courage."

It takes courage to coach. You will be rejected; you will make errors; and your job is never over. Once you have released the one you have discipled so that he or she might begin their Christian coaching career, you will be on to the next person. Finally, you must practice delayed gratification. You work for a reward that you will not attain during your lifetime. Still, regardless of the circumstances, we know that we are never alone and the reward is well worth the risk. To go to a worthy destination, and lead others there as well, Christian coaches will be called to set aside fear. It is the most important trait that we model for those we escort and an important way that we bring glory to the Lord.

Coaches Lead by Example

Someone told me a story about a dog that was hit by a car while crossing the street. Its badly injured leg was improperly set by the local veterinarian. Unfortunately thereafter, the dog walked on three legs and dragged its fourth leg behind.

Not long after that, the dog gave birth to a litter of puppies, and when the pups began to grow, the townspeople marveled at the unusual phenomenon they observed. Wherever the mother dog went, the puppies followed—each of them walking on three legs and dragging the fourth behind.

Albert Einstein said, "Setting an example is not the main means of influencing another—it is the only means." Author and activist James Baldwin agreed: "Children have never been very good at listening to their elders, but they have never failed to imitate them." That's why Paul wrote, "Now these things took place as examples for us...." (1 Corinthians 10:6 ESV).

You never know who's watching you, and you might be even more surprised to learn how your example can impact them.

Our words and actions are not like lasers, but more representative of a shotgun spraying buckshot. Depending upon our "ammunition," they can provide a shower of blessing or injury. Most people are visual learners; when they see it, they get it—coaches just need to make sure they get the right message! As Christian coaches, we need to live our lives with consciousness and intentionality—because we don't want anyone to drag a leg on account of us.

Coaches Lead from the Front

In all my years of coaching, I've never seen a leader jockeying for position at the back of the line. I've never seen a game of follow-the-leader where no one took the lead; it's just destined to go nowhere. And, I've never seen a police escort—and I've taken part in many—where the officers trailed those in the convoy.

In fact, if you attempted to place leaders in the back of any pack, they will immediately begin to reposition themselves and eventually ascend to the front. It's literally impossible to keep a good man or woman down. Leaders show the way forward and they never look back. They care about the next stop in the journey, not from where they have previously come. One thing that leaders have in common is that they prefer to be the engine rather than the caboose.

On a train, both the engine and the caboose are engaged, but only one provides the power to transport. Although scarcely seen today, at one time cabooses were prevalent, coupled on every train that rattled the tracks. Times do change, though. In the current era of railway transit, the few cabooses that remain are mostly used if a train needs to go backward. As coaches, we are to be the engine, not the caboose. We are to move forward and bring our valued passengers along for the ride.

As coaches, we need to lead from the front, not the back. As Joshua led the Israelites across the Jordan River, it was the priests who were first to step into the water. It is probably from their example that the phrase "nothing happens until you get your feet wet" originates and from which we receive a valuable leadership lesson: whether pulling a train, or an entire nation, nothing moves until we do. Christian coaches must go first!

Conclusion

While writing this book, I underwent two heart surgeries. Each reminded me that what we do today is important, because we are not promised there will be a tomorrow. But, for me, in each instance tomorrow did arrive. The immediate conclusion that I drew from this experience was that God must have more for me to accomplish. The fact that you are reading this book affirms that God isn't done with you yet, either. We are both here today because there is still work for us to do. If we think about it for a minute, why should the Lord extend our contract another day if we do not fulfill our duties today?

There are people who need our guidance. As Christian coaches, we do not allow someone to remain adrift, and we don't just point in a general direction; we provide the pull to take them there! We never give in or give out; we give them. "But you must continue to believe this truth and stand firmly in it. Don't drift away from the assurance you received when you heard the Good News" (Colossians 1:23 NLT). As one of the great coaches in history once said, "Consecrate yourselves, for tomorrow the Lord will do amazing things among you" (Joshua 3:5). We just need to wade right in.

18

TRAIN UP COACHES

"For though by this time you ought to be teachers, you need someone to teach you again the basic principles of the oracles of God. You need milk, not solid food, for everyone who lives on milk is unskilled in the word of righteousness, since he is a child. But solid food is for the mature, for those who have their powers of discernment trained by constant practice to distinguish good from evil."

Hebrews 5:12-14 ESV

Biblical Principles Work

In her book *Total Truth*, Nancy Pearcey writes: "Today the facts are in: Science itself confirms that biblical principles work in the real world—which is strong evidence that they are true."[1] Psychiatry studies have shown that those who are more religious tend to have better mental health. In addition, it's been found that religious belief leads to better physical health as well. There are "lower rates of virtually everything from cancer to hypertension to cardiovascular disease." As a matter of fact, religious people also recover quicker. "Christianity correlates with lower rates of social pathologies such as crime, drug abuse, teen pregnancy, and family breakdown."

There is not a single area where the Bible cannot enhance personal growth. And, it makes no difference whether individuals are consciously aware of their own adherence. Biblical principles work even when people do not realize that they are using them! As Christian coaches, we just need to transfer this knowledge to the VP.

The Coach's Call Sheet

One of the things I appreciated about Tim Murphy, the all-time winningest football coach at Harvard University, is that he always made me work hard on reducing the number of plays that I would take into a game. Coaches often struggle with just how many running and pass plays should be on their call sheet. If you have too few, a situation might occur in which you would find yourself unprepared to respond to your opponent's strategy. If you had too many, you might execute poorly because you did not get enough repetitions to polish each play during practice that week.

Since the NCAA limits each team to twenty hours a week of meeting and practice time, the decisions you make on play selection could make the difference between winning and losing. There has got to be a bread-and-butter list of plays that your athletes can execute flawlessly, regardless of the situation in which you call them in the game. There is a direct correlation between rehearsal, execution, and confidence. The greater the variety, the less proficient we become. Athletes must have confidence in the call, knowing it is tried and true, so they can execute it on their own.

Like any coach, you might select a different set of plays, but on my call sheet there are four biblical principles that I hope to ingrain in my VPs: Diligence, Hope, Excellence, and Practice. In the game of life, they are the staples that will provide a successful migration for the coach in training.

Diligence

Tim Notke claims, "Hard work beats talent when talent doesn't work hard."

No one has ever worked oneself out of a job, but many have lost their position due to inactivity. As we stated earlier, we work for the Lord and that means we have a duty to work hard; it's a duty that we must not relinquish. For a Christ follower, diligence is commanded and its application is better understood when we look at four components of this biblical principle:

- Communication
- Calculation
- Purpose
- Prioritization

Communication: Pass It On

Once thought of as an admirable trait, a strong work ethic now is sometimes frowned upon. Even in running races, an influx of laziness has tainted what was once considered a purely competitive realm. When a group of runners approached the starting line of any race, traditionally they have done so with the intention of performing their best, and their entrance in the event was preceded by a great deal of painstaking preparation.

Recent magazine articles highlight a disturbing trend of complacency by participants, and they even appear to advocate mediocrity where the pursuit of excellence was once the norm: "How to Finish a Race You Haven't Trained For,"[2] "How to Run a 5K Without Training at All,"[3] and "Why Having Fun is More Important Than Winning."[4]

The sports-minded Paul would disagree:

Our orders—backed up by the Master, Jesus—are to refuse to have anything to do with those among you who are lazy and refuse to work the way we taught you. Don't permit them to freeload on the rest. We showed you how to pull your weight when we were with you, so get on with it (2 Thessalonians 3:6-7 MSG).

Paul "simply wanted to provide an example of diligence, hoping it would prove contagious." So, "friends, don't slack off in doing your duty" (2 Thessalonians 3:9, 13 MSG).

Calculation

A great work ethic is not only communicable; it is calculable. The greater the amount of effort we exert, the more likely a favorable result. Not only does the Bible contend that "all hard work brings a profit, but mere talk leads only to poverty" (Proverbs 14:23), but the science community backs this assertion as well.

Robert Eisenberger, a professor of psychology at the University of Houston, studied rats and children. Eisenberger concluded that "the association between working hard and reward can be learned." Furthermore, his research found that "without directly experiencing the connection between effort and reward, both would default to laziness."[5] The correlation is a given, but coaches need additional data on their VP.

Universities usually give entrance exams, or placement tests, to assess the abilities of incoming freshmen. If these educational institutions are going to help enrollees matriculate toward a degree, they need to determine the proper curriculum for each student.

Similarly, there are multiple entry points on the discipleship pathway for those the Christian coach will guide. If you're going to help them get to the finish line, you need to know the starting point. Coaches need to calculate where the VP is on their spiritual journey, so they can craft a training program that will specifically meet their needs.

Purpose

A friend of mine used to always say, "Do everything in the natural, then trust God for the supernatural." It's a philosophy that, like Paul, expresses contentment in our current state, coupled with an acknowledgment that we must exert ourselves to improve. Paul never gave license to lethargy. His objective was to work hard, often at times to the point of exhaustion. His diligence leaves a model for us to follow: "And I have been a constant example of how you can help those in need by working hard" (Acts 20:35 NLT). But, it's not just a matter of effort; it's also about our having a worthwhile ambition.

We must pay attention, not to our own needs, but to God's agenda. Furthermore, Paul goes on to differentiate between activity and achievement. As W. Edwards Deming wisely said, "It is not enough to do your best; you must know what to do, and then do your best." We are to be busy, not busybodies. Our efforts are to be purposeful, and that is what we want to impress upon those we disciple. It's more than intentionality, because you can have good intentions and yet miss the mark.

I have never known my brother Jeff to have anything other than good intentions, but as Rev. William Nevins once said: "We judge ourselves by our intentions and others by their actions." Following the conclusion of a semester at college, on the long trip back to our parents' home, Jeff stayed overnight with his girlfriend's parents. Being the last one to leave early the next morning, Jeff was instructed to be careful as he departed so as not to accidentally let their cat outside. In the process of loading up his vehicle, Jeff noticed a cat standing just outside the door. He couldn't believe his luck. The cat could have easily scampered away and Jeff wouldn't have even known it. Breathing a sigh of relief at his good fortune, Jeff placed the cat indoors and set out for his journey home, feeling good about what had just transpired. Later that night he received a phone call from his girlfriend. Exasperatedly, she asked him why he put a stray cat in their home. She and her mother had come home to find the cat had torn the furniture and spread urine and feces throughout the house. Jeff's attempts to explain were futile and what he had once thought to be a promising relationship ended rather abruptly. Jeff's intentions were noble, but his actions were perceived otherwise. Thankfully, Jeff, and those who hear this story, now get a pretty good laugh from this incident.

As we diligently serve our Lord, the Word reminds us that our efforts will not go by unnoticed: "For God is not unjust. He will not forget how hard you have worked for him and how you have shown your love to him by caring for other believers, as you still do" (Hebrews 6:10 NLT). For the Christian coach, quality is job one and diligence is biblical principle number one.

Prioritization

Finally, we must prioritize our efforts and teach our protégés the benefit. If everything is important, nothing is important.

For the first six months as the head football coach at Charleston Southern University, I operated out of unpacked boxes. It would be two and a half years before I would hang pictures. It was a practical way of strategically applying a biblical principle: "First plant your fields; then build your barn" (Proverbs 24:27 MSG). A barn is useless if there are no crops for it to hold. A tidy and attractive-looking office in no way correlates to developing young men and winning games. On and off the field, quality required tending to matters of substance, rather than superficial items and stylistic concerns. Only in that way will growth occur and desired outcomes be achieved.

Hope: Sink or Swim

At times, I sense Christians are confused by what Paul meant when he said, "For I have learned how to be content with whatever I have" (Philippians 4:11 NLT). Pulled out of context, one might think Paul's attitude can be interpreted as indifference and likened to the "it is what it is" sentiment that all of us have articulated at one time or another. But Paul hadn't come to terms with his lot and surrendered his hope. He was not quitting. On the contrary, Paul's assertion was akin to the message he delivered to one assembly of believers, when he encouraged them to "be thankful in all circumstances" (1 Thessalonians 5:18 NLT).

Paul wasn't giving thanks for his circumstances. (Remember, he had been imprisoned, shipwrecked, rejected by those close to him, oppressed by fellow believers, had experienced poor health, was bitten by two snakes, and lived with a constant thorn in his side. He was beaten, lived in poverty and went hungry many times.) He was expressing thanks while in his current state. It was a victorious attitude that displayed emotional growth and declared an unrelenting and unfiltered trust in God.

Either out of ignorance or with intention, some accept their current position as a permanent plight. They assume a victim mentality and resign themselves to an erroneous assumption that they cannot or should not attempt to improve. They wallow in self-pity, believing that there is nothing to learn from their current condition, and in doing so, they forfeit their hope for a more prosperous tomorrow.

Hope, like any other personal attribute, must be trained— and that means there must be a trainee and a trainer. In a famous scientific experiment, a behavioral neurologist set out to determine the cause-and-effect relationship between hopelessness and perseverance by looking at the length of time a rat was able to swim.

If the test subjects were placed in water and left unattended, it would only take ten minutes before they drowned. However, if the rodents were removed from and returned to the water two to three times within those first ten minutes, they would continue to swim for more than sixty hours. With all other variables held constant, research concluded that hope, and hope alone, was the determining factor in whether the rats would sink or swim. Those with hope were able to swim 100 times longer than those without it! In matters of life and death, those with hope are best able to stay afloat.[6]

The moral from the story of Paul's life provides a life-changing lesson for us today; biblical hope breeds endurance and contentment in our lives, and it inspires others as well. It is this vital training that we pass along to those we train. When our past meets the present, there is one thing in which we can be sure; God has been there and done that. We did not sink, nor will we. He "who rescued us from so imminent a death, will do so again" and, because He is trustworthy, "we have a firm hope in Him that He will also rescue us in all the future" (2 Corinthians 1:10 WNT). One way or another, the Lord will never allow you to sink—so, just keep swimming.

Called to Excellence

Former Canadian professional golfer Stan Leonard first coined the phrase, "First we will be the best, then we will be first."

In the 1980s, Brandon Tartikoff, then president of NBC, used it as a battle cry as he led the network from last place to the number one position in primetime viewing. Since 1987, it has been the theme for my professional life and the teams I have led.

As a coach, I rarely spoke about winning; instead, I emphasized excellence. Winning, particularly in a team sport, involves factors outside of the control of any one individual. In athletics—or anything else, for that matter—the best way of avoiding defeat is to strive for excellence. Our efforts might still come up short, but we will avoid sleepless nights of wondering if the outcome would have been different had we done our best.

The synopsis for the attitude we should extend in everything we undertake is expressed particularly well in one verse: "Do your best, prepare for the worst—then trust God to bring victory" (Proverbs 21:31 MSG).

Ultimately neither victory nor defeat is in our hands, but each of us can do our best. Former Seattle Seahawks wide receiver and NFL Hall of Famer Steve Largent helped me understand that concept.

At one time, Steve Largent was the NFL record holder in career receptions, touchdowns, and receiving yards (not bad for a fourth-round draft choice!). But what intrigued me was the fact that he accomplished much of this while playing for an expansion team that struggled to find success in the early years of their existence. I asked him to what he attributed his great success. He said that, early in his playing career, the Oakland Raiders' "Commitment to Excellence" slogan captured his attention. He realized that, regardless of the score, his duty as a Christian was to not just become proficient in what he undertook, but to demonstrate excellence in each and every endeavor.

To expect anything less of ourselves, or those we coach, is to discount what we can do and diminish the One we serve.

If this biblical principle has been a core of your life and a fixture in your coaching endeavors, I congratulate you and caution you as well. "So, if you think you are standing firm, be careful that you don't fall!" (1 Corinthians 10:12). When it comes to the quest for excellence, there is no expiration date.

As one legendary football coach used to say, "Every day you either get better or you get worse. You never stay the same." Additionally, author Jim Collins, in his best-selling book *Good to Great*, warned that "good is the enemy of great." It's commendable for the common man to strive for excellence; it's a requirement for a Christ follower, and that means we must constantly improve and encourage our disciples to do the same.

Coaches set the bar. "You yourself must be an example to them by doing good works of every kind. Let everything you do reflect the integrity and seriousness of your teaching" (Titus 2:7 NLT). May the mantra of St. Jerome become the chant of our lives: "Good, better, best. Never let it rest. Till your good is better and your better is best!"

Perfect Practice Makes Perfect

Aristotle once said, "We are what we repeatedly do. Excellence then is not an act, but a habit." The repetition that he addresses, the conditioning that must occur to elicit greatness, involves much practice. Regardless of the undertaking, rehearsal is the biblical principle that provides the basis for improvement, and improvement is the pathway to expertise.

In *Outliers*[7], Malcolm Gladwell championed that repetitions, not talent or luck, are the chief cause of greatness in any endeavor. There are no "naturals" in any field. Elite performers develop primarily as the result of training in a particular skill. Gladwell calls it the "10,000–Hour Rule."

"The emerging picture from such studies is that 10,000 hours of practice is required to achieve the level of mastery associated with being a world-class expert—in anything," writes the neurologist Daniel Levitan. "In study after study, of composers, basketball players, fiction writers, ice skaters, concert pianists, chess players, master criminals, and what have you, this number comes up again and again."[8]

Practice matters, drills develop, and rehearsals have relevance! The adherence to daily disciplines reaps a reward. While the conscious mind can become tired, the subconscious does not; it continues to reinforce with every repetition.

The caveat to this assumption is known as the "Law of Fifty."[9] Theoretically, this law states that after something has been repeated fifty times, it can lose its effectiveness. For instance, a worship song can speak to the heart of the one who sings it on more than one occasion. But, after it has been sung more than fifty times, while the words are still enunciated, a disconnect begins to occur between what is being vocalized and what is internalized.

Although the 10,000–Hour Rule and the Law of Fifty appear to be polar opposites, they are actually each accurate in their own context. Something can be meaningful and lose its meaning at the same time. Our spiritual growth and skills we develop will always be meaningful. Biblical principles that are reinforced through spiritual disciplines, such as regular Bible study and prayer, will remain purposeful. But anything that becomes ritualistic has the potential to become meaningless.

In Matthew 6:7, Jesus warned against the use of "empty phrases" (ESV), "vain repetitions" (KJV), "meaningless repetition" (NASB), "babbling" (NIV). Regardless of the version read, we are cautioned against recitation; it's not a matter of the words, it's a matter of sincerity.

Just a couple of verses later, in the same chapter of Matthew (verses 9–13), Jesus gives an example of how we ought to pray. The often quoted "Lord's Prayer" is an example of a "Form Prayer." Clearly, it was a form that we are to follow as we pray, but they are not words that we are required to memorize and recite. Jesus said to pray in a similar manner; He never said that we are to pray these exact words. If that were the case, He would have discounted the very thing that He stated in Matthew 6:7.

To summarize, anything that can be memorized can remain meaningful but can become mere babbling and meaningless chatter if we do not remain focused and intentional. In these instances, our conscious mind must remain spiritually alert, so we can prevent the unintentional creation of religious "white noise."

One of the ways in which memorization can remain meaningful is when it is applied to God's Word. It's a matter of man-made versus God made. The Bible is living, active, and always relevant. When memorized, the Holy Spirit reinforces its Truth. It testifies to its own importance by saying, "All Scripture is God-breathed and is useful for teaching, rebuking, correcting and training in righteousness, so that the servant of God is thoroughly equipped for every good work" (2 Timothy 3:16-17). Its reading always reinforces and prepares the coach for the work that lies ahead.

Solomon coaches, "If the ax is dull and its edge unsharpened, more strength is needed, but skill will bring success" (Ecclesiastes 10:10). Christian coaches need to remain sharp and always maintain their edge. As Warren Weirsbe writes:

> The material sword pierces the body, but the Word of God pierces the heart. The more you use the physical sword, the duller it becomes, but using God's Word only makes it sharper in our lives. The physical sword requires the hand of the soldier, but the sword of the Spirit has its own power, for it is "living and powerful"

(Hebrews 4:12). A physical sword wounds to hurt and kill, while the sword of the Spirit wounds to heal and give life.[10]

If we want to be an excellent swordsman, we must remove our weapon from its sheath! When it comes to the Bible, no matter how you slice it, only perfect practice makes perfect. Application of biblical principles equips our disciple and ensures their spiritual growth.

19

CALL AN AUDIBLE

"I have been sent to proclaim faith to those God has chosen and to teach them to know the truth that shows them how to live godly lives."

Titus 1:1 NLT

"You hypocrite, first take the plank out of your own eye, and then you will see clearly to remove the speck from your brother's eye" (Matthew 7:5). Jesus' words from the Sermon on the Mount have been widely misinterpreted. Contrary to the opinion of many, we are our brother's keeper. We are only hypocrites if we neglect tending to our own faults and solely concentrate on those of our Christian brothers and sisters. Jesus uses hyperbole to emphasize the significance of looking inward before we look outward, but He never said we should turn a blind eye to those who might benefit from our coaching. With an unobstructed view, the Christian coach can better see how they might provide some assistance.

As a head football coach, I often told my coaching staff that we do not go out looking for problems, but we should not turn our back on them when they appear, either. It's all about motives. A Christian coach does not pass judgment, but always seeks to serve. We assess and assist; we do not critique. "There is now no condemnation for those who are in Christ Jesus" (Romans 8:1).

Christian coaches aren't just supposed to rest on their laurels, content that they have the right composition; they are to continue to develop their makeup. Just as there are things that can hijack our advancement, there are also things that can block the advancement of those we mentor. They are causes for an audible in the life of the VP. In the game of football, audibles occur whenever it becomes apparent that the action that is intended will result in a negative outcome. In this instance, athletes check out of a bad play and into a play that will work. As Christian coaches, if it becomes apparent that our disciples might be heading in the wrong direction, we have an obligation to help them turn around.

Turn, Turn, Turn

"They may look and look, yet not see; they may listen and listen, yet not understand. For if they did, they would turn to God, and he would forgive them" (Mark 4:12 GNT).

> *A disciple is about acknowledgment, attitude, and adjustment.*

A disciple is about acknowledgment, attitude, and adjustment. Disciples acknowledge that Jesus is God and profess with humble hearts that He is Lord. However, our confession is not intended to be a static, one-time event, but a dynamic and continuing lifestyle.

As in walking, Christ followers are always heading toward something and away from something else at the same time. As Christian coaches, we point our disciples in the correct direction and, if they deviate from their original pursuit, we help them to pivot. "Don't do as the wicked do, and don't follow the path of evildoers. Don't even think about it; don't go that way. Turn away and keep moving" (Proverbs 4:14-15 NLT). This is a lesson that the Christian coach has learned and one that we can impart on those we mentor. The moment we realize our disciples are facing the wrong direction, we help them execute an about-face and then keep walking. His grace and mercy instantaneously kicks in. God's promises are true. "If we confess our sins, he is faithful and just and will forgive us our sins and purify us from all unrighteousness" (1 John 1:9).

Because it is frequently referenced in Scripture, turning is a spiritual discipline that must be studied, practiced, and taught. "I have declared to both Jews and Greeks that they must turn to God in repentance and have faith in our Lord Jesus" (Acts 20:21). In chapter 26, Paul said he "started preaching this life-change—this radical turn to God and everything it meant in everyday life" (v. 20 MSG). Paul was saying that repentance was in both word and deed.

Peter concurs: "Repent, then, and turn to God, so that your sins may be wiped out, that times of refreshing may come from the Lord" (Acts 3:19). Christian coaches acknowledge that recurrent turning is a way of life for every disciple. As we drive the vehicle that transports our VPs (valuable passengers), may we demonstrate skillful application of this biblical principle, so they might one day be prepared to take the wheel.

It is a fact of life that whatever we look at, we turn toward. My motorcycle training illustrates this point. When we set out to get our learners permit, all of us were taught to be defensive drivers, but when we decide to navigate a vehicle that has two fewer wheels, the term becomes magnified. Little did our motorcycle instructor know it, but when he provided a coaching point for avoiding obstacles in our path, he equipped us with a life lesson as well. He said, "When you see an obstacle in your path, you must look somewhere else to avoid it." He went on to explain that when our eyes are fixated on the problem, we inadvertently steer toward the trouble. In like manner, if we want to avoid the pitfalls on life's road, and the collateral damage that can hurt those we transport, we must look elsewhere; we must look to Him and then train those we disciple to do the same.

There are external and internal obstacles that can disrupt the course of those we lead. Either outside variables threaten to stunt our disciple's growth or the impediments are self-imposed. In the latter case, it is the result of an incorrect perspective, a wrong attitude, or inactivity. Regardless of the interference, coaches can help their disciple steer clear of the obstruction.

External Forces: A World of Distraction

Every time we turn toward something, we turn our backs on something else. From time to time, the Christian coach might need to intervene to help the VP turn away.

Peter reminds coach and disciple alike of our objective and that which often stands in our way: "Everything that goes into a life of pleasing God has been miraculously given to us by getting to know, personally and intimately, the One who invited us to God. The best invitation we ever received! We were also given absolutely terrific promises to pass on to you—your tickets to participation in the life of God after you turned your back on a world corrupted by lust" (2 Peter 1:3-4 MSG). Many have stated that we are to live in the world, but not of the world, and coaches help VPs navigate this thin line. Our purpose is to please God, love our neighbors, and show our disciples the benefits that result when they turn their back on what the world has to offer.

Internal Forces

A New Perspective: Embracing Obstructions

While all true disciples will acknowledge the importance of turning, there are times when we must also acknowledge that some rendezvous are unavoidable. No matter how hard we try, we just cannot escape obstructions in our journey. As Christian coaches, our own experiences help us prepare disciples for the turbulence they will encounter—and sometimes the obstructions benefit us in unforeseen ways.

Following a game in Gainesville, I received a complimentary email from a Florida Gator fan. In it, they praised me for having the fortitude to hold my team in the tunnel prior to kickoff, so that the defending national champions could take the field first, thus receiving the adulation from their adoring fans. After all, it was the first home contest for the top-ranked Florida team since winning the title game versus Oklahoma in January. I thanked the fan for the kind words and went on to tell them that it was an easy decision. First, I realized the significance of the moment and it was my desire to allow the 93,000 plus fans an opportunity to honor their team. Second, there were two six foot, five inch, 250-pound Florida State troopers blocking our entrance to the stadium, so my five foot, nine inch, 170-pound frame wasn't going anywhere! After the thunderous ovation, I was more concerned about my team's attrition than their anxiousness to get to the playing surface!

Somebody once told me that the reason they give you a police escort to what is known as "The Swamp" is to make sure you do not leave. Put another way, if it were Thanksgiving, they would want to make sure the turkey reaches the table. Since at that time we were the largest underdog in the history of college football, I understood exactly where we were on the food chain. (Maybe our opponents should have

201

stationed additional troopers behind our team to prevent a mass exodus!)

Christian coaches stand in front of those they lead, but we are not there to shield them; we are there to show them. "We are guides into God's most sublime secrets, not security guards posted to protect them. The requirements for a good guide are reliability and accurate knowledge. Don't imagine us leaders to be something we aren't. We are servants of Christ, not his masters" (I Corinthians 4:2, 1 MSG). When it comes to adversity, we are to model the example of our Savior. "Since He Himself was tested and has suffered, He is able to help those who are tested" (Hebrews 2:18 HCSB). Jesus "comes alongside us when we go through hard times, and before you know it, he brings us alongside someone else who is going through hard times so that we can be there for that person just as God was there for us" (2 Corinthians 1:4 MSG). Trials are a fact of life, but like the state troopers, we as coaches are to make sure our VPs do not go unescorted. We want them to know that there is no blind side; the Lord has got them covered from every angle, and we will lead the way!

Here's the coaching point: sometimes our perspective is skewed and our observation is inaccurate. We need to let our disciples know that what they label as an obstruction might not be an obstruction at all. It might be an inconvenience, but it has been placed there for their well-being.

I wonder how many times you and I have received undue credit—or protection—because the Lord has obstructed our pathway. God is sovereign. If an impediment is before us, then by faith we must trust that it is there for a reason. For a young disciple, it will probably take more than one intervention to help them alter the lens through which they view obstacles. We can always recognize a mature disciple, because at every turn in the road there is a turn of trust.

The coach's path is a winding road. We cannot always see what is around the bend, but we place our confidence in the One who has paved the way. In circumstances like these, "cast all your anxiety on him because he cares for you" (1 Peter 5:7). For a disciple, faith in the Lord during difficult times is an acknowledgment of their saving faith, and a turn in the right direction.

Attitude Adjustments

When it comes to spiritual growth, three of the biggest issues that necessitate an audible are pride, ignorance, and inactivity. (I wish I wasn't such a great example of the first inhibitor.) In my youth, I displayed a prideful behavior that manifested itself in silence. The saying "silence is golden" has relevance if applied in the way it was intended, but in my life, that wasn't the case. In my mind, I thought asking questions was a sign of weakness. I wanted to give the impression that I knew all the answers, but as I aged, I have come to realize that I don't even know a portion of the questions.

My pride stunted my growth and was the root of many poor decisions, which crippled my ability to assist others with their spiritual development. However, when I read "You do not have because you do not ask God" (James 4:2 NIV), suddenly, I realized that it was all my own doing. I found myself lacking all because I was too proud to speak up. Since then, I have worked to rectify my wrong, so that my coaching ministry would not be rendered ineffective. Now, I kneel in reverence, respect, and when necessary, I turn in repentance. Daily I ask for wisdom and I seek counsel regularly as well. "First pride, then the crash—the bigger the ego, the harder the fall" (Proverbs 16:18 MSG). As Christian coaches, it is our responsibility to help our VPs get out of their own way, so they can avoid the crash! May humility always be the attitude of our hearts and may your disciples learn from my mistakes.

Indeed, the problem that exists in those who operate their lives in ignorance and pride is that "they are darkened in their understanding, alienated from the life of God because of the ignorance that is in them, due to their hardness of heart" (Ephesians 4:18 ESV). Our hearts must not be hardened, but remain pliable and able to be molded. When it comes to impediments to spiritual growth, we should first examine our own hearts and then invite our VPs to make the same self-assessment. Christian coaches should conduct regular checkups so we can bypass any obstruction that has blocked the spiritual artery to our hearts before the blockage causes more damage. It's one of the ways "one person sharpens another" (Proverbs 27:17). Neither of us wants to be diagnosed with heart disease.

If it's not a matter of self, then it's a matter of the shelf. Some disciples have progressed on their walk but become incapacitated somewhere along the way. Either they believe that they have "arrived" and that they have attained a certain status or some magical age where it is no longer necessary to grow, or they have become wayward during their discipleship journey. These individuals have put their faith, as well as the Bible, on the shelf. As Christian coaches, part of our role is to help them retrieve it.

It is our duty to "restore that person gently. But watch yourselves, or you also may be tempted" (Galatians 6:1). If our VP is on a self-imposed exile, we need to help them re-"turn" to the right path. If those we mentor get out of their own way and don't put their faith on a shelf, then they will always be attached to the source of infinite knowledge and ready to be empowered.

20

EMPOWER COACHES

"You're well–constructed upon Him....Now do what you've been taught. School's out; quit studying the subject and start living it!"

Colossians 2:7 MSG

Coaching is about transferring a message and a skill set for the benefit of the recipient and those they influence. We mentor others to multiply ourselves, so that our ministry might grow exponentially. However, if those we disciple are always relying on us and never learn to function for themselves, then our ministry will come to an end when we do. This was the painful lesson that was learned by George Whitefield.

Although his name is seldom recognized today, during the 18th century Whitefield was well known throughout Britain and in the American colonies. As an evangelist and preacher, George Whitefield traveled extensively to share the gospel, and his eloquent sermons impacted countless lives. Along with his contemporary, John Wesley, the founder of Methodism, George Whitefield played an integral role in a Protestant movement that became known as the Great Awakening.

The significance of this revival is well established in historical record, but each man's efforts are remembered differently. John Wesley's contributions have extended to this day, while George Whitefield's efforts have largely faded into obscurity. Here's why: Whitefield failed to disciple those he led to Christ. Although he was a tremendous evangelist, by not investing in the spiritual growth of his VPs, he failed to give traction to his ministry.

In his later years, Whitefield recognized the error he had made and he foresaw the ramifications: "My brother Wesley acted wisely. The souls that were awakened under his ministry he joined in class, and thus preserved the fruits of his labor. This I neglected, and my people are a rope of sand." To paraphrase Kenneth J. Collins, "Let this be a warning for (those) who only evangelize the lost, but never disciple the found." Sooner or later, each of us will leave the mission field. To extend our influence, Christian coaches must empower others so they can add to our work. Coaches need to tutor others so our ministry does not die with us.

Coaches Provide Tutoring

The best tutoring occurs when it is done one-on-one. After all, "We didn't learn this by reading books or going to school; we learned it from God, who taught us person-to-person through Jesus," and as Christian coaches, our duty is to let those we lead know that "we're passing it on to [them] in the same firsthand, personal way" (1 Corinthians 2:13 MSG). It is certainly preferable to the alternative—trial and error.

One of the better stories I've heard to illustrate this point was told to me by Bob Trenor, a former assistant athletic director at Charleston Southern University. After I became head football coach, he and I embarked on a customary trip to introduce me to some key boosters and allow me an opportunity to speak at a few gatherings in an area of South Carolina known as the Low Country. During one leg of our excursion, he shared a story from his youth about an adventurous friend who had an obvious bent for thrill-seeking.

The story goes as follows: One day, as they were walking home from school, they paused on a bridge on a small rural road. As they looked down from atop the bridge, they noticed a number of alligators congregating in the river below. Bob's friend said, "Watch this!" and, without hesitating, he jumped directly into the group of gators below. Bob watched, mortified and slightly intrigued, as the alligators all quickly swam away. When he emerged from the water, Bob asked his friend, "Why in the world would you do that? Weren't you afraid?" His friend went on to explain to him that alligators would only attack if they were nesting or in mating season. Bob replied, "How did you know that it wasn't nesting or mating season?" To which his friend nonchalantly answered, "They swam away, didn't they?" Bob swears that this is a true story, and he and I both swear that his friend is nuts!

In tutoring those we mentor, Christian coaches do not resort to trial and error. Unlike Bob's friend, we "don't have to rely on the world's guesses and opinions" (1 Corinthians 2:11 MSG). Coaches craft customized plans that carefully guide disciples through successive stages meant to lead them to graduation.

There is a Ticket to Ride, But This is No Ride Along

Though there may be a season in which we carry the VP, it is really a misnomer to call the one we transport a "valued passenger." They are not just coming along for the ride; sooner or later, they must learn how to pitch in. Like stages in the maturation process, transportation of a person can be separated into four phases: birth, infancy, adolescence, and adulthood. With parental supervision, early stages of the journey might require more attentiveness on behalf of the coach. The VP might stand for "valued passenger" at the onset, but eventually VP will stand for "valued participant" as they advance and begin to provide contribution.

In their book *A Passionate Life*, Michael Breen and Walt Kallestad state that there are four stages in the growth of a new disciple[1]:

- I Do; You Watch—In this initial stage, the coach gives clear direction to the coach-in-training. The mentor serves as the illustration that the mentee will likely mimic.
- I Do; You Help—In this phase, the student is invited to participate in the transportation process. As the disciple begins to cut their teeth, the coach stands ready to assist by providing encouragement and instruction as requested.
- You Do; I Help—This phase is marked by transition; the pupil becomes greater, while the instructor becomes lesser. The relationship between the coach and his prodigy changes from leader/follower to personal partnership.
- You Do; I Watch—In this final stage, transference is complete; the coach now separates from their mentee. The coach and the new coach will now seek to replicate the process in others. The coach extends his coaching tree, while the disciple seeks to sprout the first branch of their own tree.

Breen and Kallestad's model is demonstrated by Christ, supported in Scripture, and the method that we, Christian coaches, seek to employ in the training of a new coach.

Interval Training

In athletics, interval training occurs when a coach alternately increases and decreases an activity's level of intensity. For instance, when a coach conditions an athlete, the coach might intermittently change the pace of the run from a sprint to a jog, and vice versa —and repeat the aerobic exchange until the exercise has concluded. Sometimes, the athlete will know when the change will occur, and other times they do not. Since life also has an ebb and flow, Christian coaches need to train their disciples to adapt similarly. We don't immediately release those under our tutelage, and we don't subject them to constant pressure, but we do turn it up a notch for brief intervals. To prepare those we lead to stand alone, coaches will:

- Supervise the Transition
- Elevate the Challenge
- Turn over the Reins
- Point Elsewhere

Supervise the Transition: Trust and Verify

Paul writes: "Practice these things, immerse yourself in them, so that all may see your progress" (1 Timothy 4:15 ESV).

In transferring any message, there's an important coaching point that all coaches understand: if you can teach it, you know it. As a coach, I knew that if I was the only one who lectured my team, eventually they would tune me out. However, if they knew that I might hand them the marker, so they might diagram and explain a play to their teammates, they tended to remain focused. Periodically, and without warning, I would put my athletes "on the board." I trusted my athletes to do their homework, but I verified it as well.

If the one you mentor knows testing might occur, they will be better prepared for the exhibition. Before they go it alone, Christian coaches provide a safe arena in which their disciples might practice. This method of training also enables the coach to assess how successful they have been in transferring their message to their pupil. To reinforce one point that was made earlier, "It's not what you know, but what they know that counts," so coaches need to find out what those they lead know. If an adjustment needs be made, it's better to do it early, so our VP does not compound their error.

Elevate the Challenge

Legendary coach John Wooden warned, "Do not let what you cannot do interfere with what you can do."

Occasionally, coaches must crank up the intensity to see those we disciple continue to make strides. Years ago, a friend led me where did not want to go, so I could get to where I needed to be. We were skiing at a resort near Boise, Idaho, when he suggested we take a lift to an area of the mountain with which I was unfamiliar. I was apprehensive, but I agreed to go along as long as he did not lead me down a difficult slope. At the time, I only felt comfortable on intermediate trails and I had no intention of progressing beyond these "Blue" runs. Although my friend assured me that he would not take me down any "Black Diamond" routes, he took me there nonetheless. (It was my fault entirely—I trusted him!)

When there's only one way to go and in this case, one way down, you don't have much of a choice. Surprisingly, I skied the route without falling. Since that time, I have skied a number of "Black Diamonds," but I might not have done so, had he not guided me there. There are two coaching points from this experience. First, steeper grades are more challenging, but they can be more exciting as well. The greater the risk, the greater the reward.

As a Christian coach, to advance those under our care, sometimes we need to take them to the next level. After all, how can someone know that they "can do everything through Christ, who gives [them] strength" (Philippians 4:13), unless they are stretched to do something they previously thought undoable? Second, don't always believe what your friends tell you! They might have ulterior motives.

Tutoring is scripted. I didn't know it was coming, but my friend certainly did! The lesson plan he employed was probably a spur-of-the-moment decision, but that's typically not how a good coach operates. Coaches take great care to lay out lesson plans to ensure that all bases are covered. They orchestrate scenarios that they believe are most likely to present themselves in a game and replicate them in practice so their athletes are prepared. Every once in a while coaches surprise them so they remain poised when unpredictable events occur—but even then the surprise was scripted.

Turn Over the Reins

Occasionally, coaches need to shake things up. Sometimes, we need to turn over the coaching reigns to others—at least temporarily. I didn't do it often, but I have pulled my coaches out of practice and left my team on the field without coaching supervision (and I've abandoned a meeting a time or two or as well). But it was staged, an intentional action designed to inspire those left to step up, to lead themselves and their teammates. Sometimes, one of the players was in on it. Prayerfully, I utilized this strategy if I sensed that things had become stagnant and I believed something dramatic needed to happen to reinvigorate the troops.

If I felt we were lacking leadership, I put them in a position where they must fend for themselves—and they always did. These young men took over the practice or meeting and their teammates supported them each time. I knew they could do it, but I needed them to find that out for themselves. Additionally, I wanted them to pull for each other and prop up their leaders, so that they would work together to achieve victory. To succeed, a team must "be completely united, with only one thought and one purpose" (1 Corinthians 1:10 GNT). They needed to know what it felt like to be on their own before they were ever alone. Coaches won't always stand next to them; eventually the game will begin and coaches will be forced to the sidelines while our team fends for themselves.

My point is this: we can't forever run alongside someone who is learning to ride a bike. We help them hit stride, and then we watch them go. If we need to leave the field, to sever the umbilical cord, or take them to the edge of a cliff to show them that they can descend it alone, so be it. After all, Jesus sent His apostles on a mission trip by themselves (Matthew 10), and He sent them unaccompanied in a boat that would encounter a storm (Matthew 14:22-36). Coaches provide whatever one-on-one tutoring is needed. Christian coaches make disciples who make disciples. And we do that by preparing our VPs for our absence.

Point Elsewhere

As my children grew, I knew they would reach an age where they did not listen with the same attentiveness they did as adolescents. That's right—I knew they would become teenagers! Knowing this, I planned accordingly. While they were still young and mindful to my instruction, I would direct their attention to individuals who possessed the character traits I wanted them to embrace. If they were going to seek another role model, I wanted to point them in the right direction.

Although we should strive to lead by example, coaches cannot be the sole prototype for those we mentor. There are limits to what you're able to do. First, we will not always be present. If our disciples are visual learners, we need to help them identify where else their vision should be cast. Second, everyone has a hole, but when we align with others, we can be whole. When we work alongside others, we can camouflage our weaknesses and accent our strengths. Good coaches draft off others so we do not inadvertently drag our VPs down; we procure their help even if they are not aware of it.

Here's the bottom line and another key coaching point regarding those you mentor: who cares how they get the message, as long as they get the message. A coach knows when to lead and when to step aside. In fact, when working with a group, an athletic team or any other, if someone other than the group's leader speaks similarly, it only magnifies the voice of the leader. Unity of message is a powerful vehicle for VP transportation. The old adage is true: there is strength in numbers, and that strength is amplified when there are more people echoing the leader's words and emulating the leader's actions.

Separation

I come from a family of farmers, so I know what it means to sow; it means to distribute to fertile soil. Seedlings cannot germinate if they are kept in the bag. Christian coaches will never produce maximum yield unless they take the crop of coaches they have cultivated and distribute them elsewhere. Whenever I have hired someone I have told them that I did not expect them to retire in that position; eventually, I expected them to move on. If they did a good job, I would help plant them in another field. It always hurts to lose a good coach, but we cannot increase crop production if we keep them to ourselves. If they stayed, they would also limit our ability to develop new coaches.

Over the years, I have maintained contact with a number of my former assistant coaches, but I certainly am not as engaged as I was when they were on my staff. When asked, I provide counsel and serve as a reference for them as they look to expand their coaching careers, and I pray for them more than they realize. I transported them as best I could through stages of development and then I empowered them so they could plant their own coaching tree.

21

FINISH STRONG

"I declare today that I have been faithful. If anyone suffers eternal death, it's not my fault, for I didn't shrink from declaring all that God wants you to know."

(Acts 20:26-27 NLT)

A Fighting Spirit

We have always been inspired by those who live a bold existence—heroes. Sales of books increase and movies set box office records when tales of heroism are the centerpiece of their story. *Gladiator, Braveheart,* and *Rocky* are some of my personal favorites and just a few of the examples that come to mind. Whether a factual account or mythical legend, the common theme of each narrative is that the hero—or heroine—didn't shrink. They answered the call; they fulfilled their purpose. And, often, it came at great cost. There are concluding lessons for Christian coaches and the first one is this: to finish well you must remain strong. "Run when you can, walk if you have to, crawl if you must, just never give up" (Dean Karnazes). A second lesson is that every one of us has the potential to be a hero.

Michelle Perea is one of my heroes. Michelle, her husband, Mike, and their four children have been a part of

215

Southwinds Church in Tracy, California, for over a decade. In October 2007, Michelle received devastating news. She was diagnosed with sarcoma, an extremely rare form of cancer, and told she had two months to live. Five surgeries and over a decade later, Michelle is living proof that with God all things are possible. When I read Paul's comments in Philippians 3:10, I think about Michelle: "I gave up all that inferior stuff so I could know Christ personally, experience his resurrection power, be a partner in his suffering, and go all the way with him to death itself" (MSG). Michelle has suffered a great deal—her body has been ravaged through the ordeal—but her faith has never wavered. She is going all the way with Jesus Christ.

Baseball great Babe Ruth said, "It's hard to beat a person who never gives up." Years ago, I developed an acronym to describe people who personify uncommon perseverance. I call them S.T.U.D.s (meaning they Stand Tough Under Duress). Michelle is a S.T.U.D. There are two types of people in the world: bystanders and participants. Michelle has chosen to be the latter. Each spring, she participates in the American Cancer Society's Relay for Life. It's a worldwide event designed to raise funds for research grants and programs for the detection, treatment, and prevention of cancer. The steps she takes around the track are often physically—and sometimes emotionally—painful, but she walks nonetheless. She's become a fixture at the event and a visible inspiration for all in attendance.

Even though some the medical community had written her off nearly 14 years ago, God was not done with Michelle yet; He had a lot more for her to do. She had people to coach: family, friends, and everyone she met. She partnered with Christ every day and served as a team builder in her community. I cannot count the number of times that I've prayed that God would remove the defective parts in me so that only Jesus would remain. Literally, because they have been rendered defective by cancer, surgeons removed numerous body parts from Michelle. Her physique became more and more diminutive, but to me, she was larger-than-life and of this I was always certain: she has not, and will not, ever shrink!

My dear friend has gone to be with the Lord, but I'm proud to be one of the many branches on her very large coaching tree.

Essentials for the Journey: A Compass, A Map, and A GPS

A few years back, I read *StrengthFinder 2.0*[1] and took the test that was included in the book's appendix. The test was designed to identify which of the thirty-four strengths identified in the book most closely matched that of the person taking the test. Although the premise was that everyone has five predominant strengths, my contention is that all Christian coaches exhibit the one known as "Futuristic." I define futuristic as the ability to forecast the future and then implement a strategy that will optimizes our chances to reach that end. We know the end game. It's that we would become a fully devoted follower of Jesus Christ, that we would glorify God in all we do, and that we would help others do likewise.

Once the objective is understood, the futuristic person then collects the resources needed to make the journey and then sequentially orders their steps so that they might arrive at the intended target in the most advantageous manner. As a review of what is needed for the excursion upon which we are about to embark, we remind ourselves of the resources that a coach must collect as he sets out on his spiritual journey: a compass, a map, and a GPS.

The shortest distance between two points is a straight line (when you have a math teacher for a father, you learn this principle at a young age). The ripple in our journey should relate to the effect our walk has on others, not a wavelike trajectory due to our inconsistent travel in the plotted course we take on the discipleship pathway. Proverbs reiterates this axiom: "Trust God from the bottom of your heart; don't try to figure out everything on your own. Listen for God's voice in everything you do, everywhere you go; he's the one who will keep you on track" (3:5-6 MSG). When we map out a path, we generally take the course with the fewest deviations possible. If a reroute occurs on our journey, it means we have lost our way or a better route becomes available. In either case, a compass, map, and GPS prove to be essential as we travel.

The longer the trip, the greater our need for continued direction. To finish strong, we need to start and remain strong. As Christ followers, we always know where to turn to get our bearings: "But you have received the Holy Spirit, and he lives within you, so you don't need anyone to teach you what is true. For the Spirit teaches you everything you need to know, and what he teaches is true—it is not a lie. So, just as he taught you, remain in fellowship with Christ" (1 John 2:27 NLT). Truth is the Word and Truth is a person—Christ Jesus. It is a relationship that will keep us on track and the truth we must not trade.

If the church is the driver and the coach the vehicle, then Christ is the compass upon which we direct our course and the only hope we have of reaching our destination. Jesus reminds us of that fact when He states that "apart from me you can do nothing" (John 15:5). The Holy Spirit keeps us attached to the power source and shows us the way to immortality. When we "wade right in," we are not to just flounder and splash about. There is to be intentionality in all we do. Like the priests who led the Israelites across the Jordan River and into the Promised Land, when we step into the water, we are to clear a path and show the way.

In the book of Proverbs, the words "path" and "way" are found nearly one hundred times (NKJV). There is obviously some point the Lord is trying to get across through the constant repetition of these two words, and His meaning is not lost on those who proclaim Him as Lord. The way is both a path and a person! In Hebrew, the "way" means the moral quality and orientation of our life. It is the process that leads to the progress of becoming like Christ. There is a path to follow and a model to emulate: Jesus. Peter makes this clear to us when he says, "To this you were called, because Christ suffered for you, leaving you an example that you should follow in his steps" (1 Peter 2:21). Christian coaching declares that there is a new way and path to get there. It is not just a philosophical ideal; its concepts lead to practical steps. Whether the road be rough or the pathway smooth, our quest should be to become transformed into Christ's image, as we transport others to the finish line.

When I think of following in one's steps, I reminisce about tracking through the snow as a child behind my dad. With each step, I would carefully step into the footprint that he left as he led the way. This maneuver made my walk more productive and his lead gave me direction. My dad did not just initiate my life; he also guided me in a training process that transported me into maturity. He was my coach and I was his valued person (and I wasn't the only VP placed in his charge). So there is no confusion or resentment, my dad used to tell everyone that each of his four boys was his favorite. Isn't that how a good coach should make each of his VPs feel?

Each of you are a favorite son or daughter of your Heavenly Father. Salvation through Christ is not just an entry point; it is the start of the journey. Like my father's imprint in the snow, it is the first step along a new trail. Jesus is the beginning, the end, and the means to the end. No matter how and when He appears, from start to finish, Jesus is the one common denominator in each believer's travelogue.

Whether it be for a season or lifetime, God the Father makes Himself known in many ways and in many names. Jesus has many aliases as well, but He is never incognito. Those who try to remain inconspicuous sometimes attempt to conceal their identity. But not Jesus. Jesus is the real deal, and He never masks Himself so that He cannot be recognized. He has many personas so He can connect with a vast number of people in a variety of ways. For example, in the first chapter of the book of John alone, the author gives seven distinct names for Jesus. No matter what name you give Him, only Jesus is the Way and He has been showing us the Way from the dawn of creation.

God's Word has served as a road map since the days of the exodus of the Israelites from Egypt to their entrance into the Promised Land. The Word was foundational, fundamental, and essential on their journey. On the road today, with regard to the Bible, we would be well advised to follow the American Express slogan: "Don't leave home without it!"

It's not enough that we possess a map; we must also know how to read it. All maps have a "visual hierarchy" as part of their illustration. They give helpful hints as we progress on our pathway. The larger the print, the more dramatic the font, the more prominent the highlight, and the more attention we should pay to it. In this life, we need more than our good judgment to successfully proceed. To fully comprehend the clues intended to help us navigate we need divine guidance. The Holy Spirit helps us understand the map.

Paul shares that the Spirit interprets what God has freely given us (1 Corinthians 2:12), and He wants us to understand that there is an established blueprint to plot our course. Not only does God provide direction free of charge, Jesus says that the Spirit will "guide you into all truth" (John 16:13). We do not receive a partial set of instructions; we have access to it all. The Spirit serves as a virtual GPS (God's Positional System), revealing what God wants to share with us, so that we might understand our next step. This dependency ensures that the disciple and those who are branches on our coaching tree stay on the narrow path, always looking for clues that will advance us toward the end of the line. The Christian coach is the Lord's chosen emissary to get the job done. Regardless the task, no job is too big and no job is too small. We realize there is a cost for discipleship and we agree to pay the price each day of our lives.

When I look at the discipleship path, I do not see those who are present, but those who are not; they are conspicuous in their absence. As Christian coaches, we must invite others to join us on our journey and then lead those who follow us on the correct path. Whether our relationship with the VP is personal or professional, it is not by accident you are in their lives. "God the Father knew you and chose you long ago" (1 Peter 1:2 NLT) for these divine appointments. This is your hour; this is your day. It is not by accident, but strategic design that you have been chosen "for such a time as this" (Esther 4:14). What you do today matters, because the future is just a series of here and now moments strung together over time.

It is not about what you have done in the past or what you have known; it is about where you go from here. It's *Game On!* You and I have a promising future and valid reason for a bright outlook on an ever-emerging trail. We have a compass, a map, and a GPS for life's journey, and the resolve to finish strong. "Therefore, since God in his mercy has given us this new way, we never give up" (2 Corinthians 4:1 NLT). Christian coaches do not remain stationary; with our game plan in hand, we are always on the move....Onward, Outward, and Upward! Whatever we do and wherever the Lord leads, when we one day reach His throne may we proudly exclaim: "I didn't shrink!"

APPENDIX

MILLS FAMILY CONSTITUTION

We, the Mills Family, here declare on this day, and solemnly swear to abide by, the following articles as we commit ourselves together to honor, love, and respect one another through the good and challenging times to the best of our ability.

Article I   We Will Honor God
II Corinthians 5:7; Galatians 2:20 – 21; Hebrews 10:25; II Timothy 2:15; Matthew 22:37; Romans 12:9 – 21

A. We are committed to living by faith and not by sight. We realize faith in God requires action, action requires a decision, and the decision is most difficult during a tough circumstance.
B. We are committed to attending church and church-related functions regularly to grow spiritually, encourage the church body, and serve as we are called.
C. We are committed to daily devotional time where we will individually develop a relationship with our Heavenly Father through prayer and the study of His Word.
D. We commit to loving the Lord with all our hearts, souls, and minds. We will strive to make Him our priority and demonstrate our love by obeying His commandments.

E. We are committed to living our lives as His servants, testifying to the gospel of God's grace, sharing His plan of salvation, and exemplifying Christ-like traits. We will confess our sins and repent from those words, thoughts, and actions which cause Him to be removed from the throne of our lives. We will love others, forgive and pray for those who have wronged us, and understand that everyone is a creature of God and deserves our respect.

Article II   We Will Honor Our Family
Philippians 3:12 – 14; 4:8, 13

A. We are committed to supporting, encouraging, loving, respecting, and praising each other. We will share each other's joy and sorrow and demonstrate loyalty to one another by keeping the individual's and the family's confidence.
B. We are committed to honoring our father and mother. While we have the right to ask questions, we recognize and will submit to their God-given authority while exhibiting a proper attitude.
C. We will demonstrate our dedication to one another by attending important events/activities of each person whenever possible. After the Lord, our family is the most important priority in our lives.
D. We are committed to respecting each other's privacy and things. We will show good stewardship by taking care of our family's home and possessions.

Article III   We Will Develop Outstanding Character
James 1: 2 – 4; Galatians 6:9; James 1:12; Matthew 25:21; Luke 6:31; Proverbs 18:8; II Timothy 1:7; lesions 1:10; Colossians 3:23 – 24; Philippians 4:12

A. We are committed toward displaying courage, confidence, and determination by persevering through the challenges that occur in life. We will not feel self-pity but will demonstrate persistence as we live each day and foster an optimistic outlook that looks forward to the day, we will be made full and complete, not lacking anything.

B. We are committed to living a life of integrity. We will make correct ethical and moral decisions. We will operate with complete honesty, thus making our word our bond. We will not gossip, but only speak positively of others.

C. We are committed to having a positive attitude. While we recognize emotions to events may cause us to initially react negatively, we will choose to respond positively shortly thereafter. Our attitude will reflect the confidence in our God-given abilities, thankful hearts for our many blessings, and sensitivity toward those who are hurting.

D. We are committed to living a disciplined life. We will show maturity by delaying gratification until a proper time. We are selfless in our endeavors and content in the environment we have been placed by God.

We are committed to striving for excellence in every aspect of our lives. Our ability is God-given, but how we utilize that ability is our gift to God. We will not pursue worldly recognition, but heavenly acknowledgment as we aspire to hear, "well done thy good and faithful servant.

NOTES

Chapter 2

1. World's Most Valuable Thrift Store Finds, http://www.giveitlove.com/the-worlds-most-valuable-thrift-store-and-garage-sale-finds/2/?safari=1 (accessed May 18, 2018).

Chapter 4

1. Angela Duckworth (2016) *Grit, The Power and Passion of Perseverance*, New York: Scribner

Chapter 5

1. Bill McCartney (1995), *Ashes from Glory*, Nashville: Thomas Nelson
2. CBN News, "Tim Tebow's Shocking Story About John 3:16 'Coincidence' Goes Viral", January 7, 2018, http://www1.cbn.com/cbnnews/entertainment/2018/january/tim-tebow-rsquo-s-nbsp-shocking-story-about-john-3-16-lsquo-coincidence-rsquo-goes-viral (accessed May 16, 2018).

Chapter 6

1. http://cusefca.org/about/ (accessed November 7, 2018)

2. Nancy Pearcey (2004) *Total Truth,* Wheaton: Crossway
3. Why 3% of Harvard MBAs Make Ten Times as Much as the Other 97% Combined, https://sidsavara.com/why-3-of-harvard-mbas-make-ten-times-as-much-as-the-other-97-combined/, (Accessed January 1, 2020)
4. Mark Batterson (2014), *The Grave Robber,* Grand Rapids: Baker Books
5. Arien Mack and Irv Rock, (1998). Inattentional Blindness, MIT Press

Chapter 7

1. Keri Lynn Engel "Wilma Rudolph, Olympic gold medalist & civil rights pioneer." Amazing Women in History. (2012, August 14) (accessed November 10, 2019) http://www.amazingwomeninhistory.com/wilma-rudolph-olympic-gold-medalist-civil-right-pioneer/
2. Wikipedia contributors, "History of polio," *Wikipedia, The Free* Encyclopedia, https://en.wikipedia.org/w/index.php?title=History_of_polio&oldid=930023774 (accessed January 2, 2020).

Chapter 8

1. Dr. Wayne Grudem, (1999) *Bible Doctrine,* Grand Rapids: Zondervan

Chapter 9

1. Wikipedia contributors, "Patrick Beckert," https://en.wikipedia.org/w/index.php?title=Patrick_Beckert&oldid=833103757 (accessed November 7, 2019)
2. Shield and "Veritas" History, http://www.hcs.harvard.edu/~gsascf/shield-and-veritas-history/ (Accessed November 25, 2019)
3. Angela Duckworth (2016) *Grit, The Power and Passion of Perseverance*, New York: Scribner
4. Wikipedia contributors,"Heroin,"https://en.wikipedia.org/w/index.php?title=Heroin&oldid=838271142 (accessed November 25, 2019)

Chapter 10

1. Kathleen Elkman, The single most effective way to get rich, according to a 90-year-old personal-finance classic, December 14, 2015 http://www.businessinsider.com/pay-yourself-first-2015-12 (accessed May 16, 2018).
2. Steve Ferrar, (1990) *Point Man*, Colorado Springs: Multnomah Books

Chapter 11

1. Leon Stier (March 2018) "You Christians Are Crazy" March 28, 2018, https://emailmeditations.wordpress.com/2018/03/28/1812-you-christians-are-crazy/ (accessed May 18, 2018).

Chapter 13

1. Charles Stanley, "Life Principle 6: The Principle of Sowing and Reaping: You reap what you sow, more than you sow, and later than you sow", July 6, 2014, https://www.intouch.org/read/life-principle-6-the-principle-of-sowing-and-reaping (accessed May 18, 2018).
2. Wikipedia contributors, "Hamburger Helper," *Wikipedia, The Free Encyclopedia*, https://en.wikipedia.org/w/index.php?title=Hamburger_Helper&oldid=818192245 (accessed May 15, 2018).
3. John Maxwell, January 14, 2015 https://www.johnmaxwell.com/blog/it-all-comes-down-to-what-you-do-daily/ (accessed January 2, 2020).

Chapter 14

1. Tony Carnes, "From Pepper Street Gang to Glorious Brooklyn: Jackie Robinson's Faith Journey." A Journey Through NYC Religions. April 10, 2016, http://www.nycreligion.info/pepper-street-gang-glorious-brooklyn-jackie-robinsons-faith-journey/ (accessed May 15, 2018).

Chapter 15

1. Emma Green (June 2017) "Bernie Sanders' Religious Test for Christians in Public Office" June 8, 2017, https://www.theatlantic.com/politics/archive/2017/06/bernie-sanders-chris-van-hollen-russell-vought/529614/ (accessed May 18, 2018).

Chapter 17

1. Chambliss, Daniel F. (1989). The mundanity of excellence: An ethnographic report on stratification and Olympic swimmers. *Sociological Theory* 7 (1):70-86.

Chapter 18

1. Nancy Pearcey (2004) *Total Truth*, Wheaton: Crossway
2. Anna Medaris Miller, "How To Finish A Race You Haven't Trained For", November 12, 2014, https://health.usnews.com/health-news/health-wellness/articles/2014/11/12/how-to-finish-a-race-you-havent-trained-for (accessed May 18, 018).
3. Alexa Tucker, "How To Run A 5k Without Training At All", June 17, 2016, https://www.self.com/story/how-to-run-a-5k-without-training-at-all (accessed May 18, 2018).
4. Angela Horn "Why Having Fun Is More Important Than Winning", December 24, 2017, https://www.care2.com/greenliving/why-having-fun-is-more-important-than-winning.html (accessed May, 18, 2018).
5. Robert Eisenberger (1989) *Blue Monday: The Loss of the Work Ethic in America*, New York: Paragon House
6. Joseph T. Hallinan "The Remarkable Power of Hope", May 7, 2014, https://www.psychologytoday.com/us/blog/kidding-ourselves/201405/the-remarkable-power-hope
7. Gladwell, Malcolm (2008) *Outliers, The Story of Success*, New York: Little, Brown and Company

8. Gladwell, Malcolm (2008) *Outliers, The Story of Success*, New York: Little, Brown and Company
9. Rick Warren (2012) *The Purpose Driven Life*, Grand Rapids: Zondervan
10. Wiersbe, Warren (2003) *Be Confident, A New Testament Study on Hebrews*, Colorado Springs: Chariot Victor

Chapter 20

1. Mike Breen & Walt Kallestad (2005) *A Passionate Life,* Colorado Springs: Nexgen

Chapter 21

1. Tom Rath (2007), *StrengthsFinder 2.0*, Omaha: Gallup Press

BOOK LAUNCH TEAM

A very special thank you to the following who played an important role in helping kickoff *Game On!*

Dick and Sherry Arbuckle
John Balbin
Steve Barrows
Daryl Blair
Kristi and James Bingham
Scott Bolton
Brett Bowdren
Christine and Mark Bronson
Meredith Brown
Randy Burns
Kevin Canterbury
Nick Carnes
Ron and Michele Carson
Solmaz Chadwell
John Cleveland
Judy and John Cleveland
Rudy Costa
Darrell Coulter
Jennifer Dabalos
Adrienne Doppee
Pam and John Drafts
Olivia Egnor
James Enos
Paul Francis
Jennifer and Logan Francisco
Robin Fuller

John Goulding
Sue Ann Greene
Michael and Ceci Haas
Skip Hall
Brad Harrison
Rhonda Harvey
Bob Hines
Leslie and Dain Hunter
Lynda Ives
Toby Jacobi
Dianne Jones
Ron Joseph
Dave and Dara Kazakevich
Gloria and Matt Knaus
Gian Lemmi
Terry Lemon
Eric Lethco
Rich Linden
Roger Lipe
Summer Lopez
Bobby Lutes
Marko Marin
Ian McCaw
Steve McDonald
Don McNely
Jan Mills

Jeff Mills

Jerry Mills

Joby Mills

Tim Murray

Mark and Wende Myers

Alex Neicu

Sherie Neitzel

Eric Nielsen

Risa Oglesby

Larry Owen

Roger Owen

Dave Padilla

Mike Perea

Sophia Perea

Allen Peterson

Kimmie Pitcock

Stephanie Quezada

Mickey Rainwater

Veronica Rico

Neil Rose

Lisa Sellers

Keith Sharp

Chelsea and Chadd Sheffield

Matthew Smiley

Mike Sorg

Wally Sparks

Brian and Errolyn Springer

Jim Staton

Tim and Pam Steger

Mary Sundblad

Kavita Taylor

Chris Thielen

Ron Thomson

James Tower

Gary Vargyas

Gary and Gloria Vierra

Wayne Villaluna

Kyle Vital

Toni Wiemers

Frank Williamson

Don Woodall

Peter Young

ABOUT THE AUTHOR

Jay Mills is from a family of coaches, and he, himself, spent thirty years coaching college football (thirteen of which as a head coach). Coach Mills served at premier institutions like Notre Dame and Harvard and was mentored by some of the greatest coaches of our generation, such as Lou Holtz. Jay has taught a university course on coaching motivation, received the Mike Campbell Lifetime Achievement award for his coaching career, and even had the pleasure of coaching a Heisman winner.

As a head coach at a Christian university for a decade, he successfully integrated biblical principles as part of a whole person development model with his team. Since then, he has personally transferred the coaching skill set into ministry and, because all Christ followers are, in actuality, ministers, his experience has assisted them in achieving similar results.

In addition to serving in his current role as an ordained pastor, Jay is also an author, motivational speaker, and inspiring writer, who produces a popular monthly newsletter ("Coaching Points") and video series ("Chalk Talks"). These resources focus on biblically based coaching principles for personal and professional growth – – and they're provided free of charge. Visit his website (coachjaymills.com) or call (270) 244 – 5005 to subscribe to these resources and learn how you can bring Jay to your next event.

Stay up-to-date with the latest resources from Coach Jay Mills!

To subscribe to Jay's free CoachingPoints newsletter and ChalkTalk video series, text **CJM** to **33777**. For more information, visit **coachjaymills.com.**